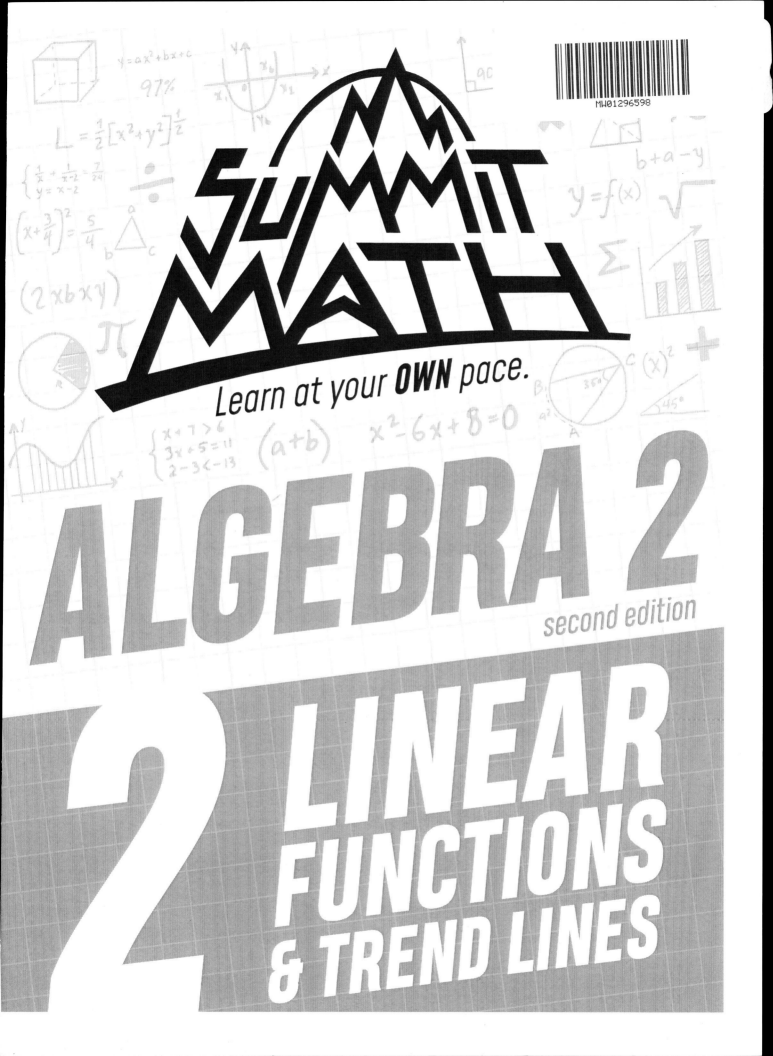

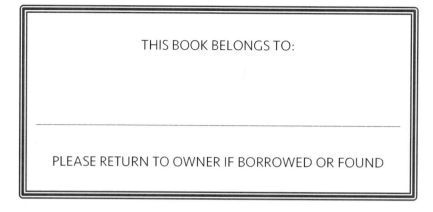

PLEASE RETURN TO OWNER IF BORROWED OR FOUND

DEDICATION
To Lauren, Chloe, Dawson and Teagan

ACKNOWLEDGEMENTS
I started writing these books in 2013 to help my students learn better. I kept writing them because I received encouraging feedback from students, parents and teachers. Thank you to all who have used these books, pointed out my mistakes, and made suggestions along the way. Thank you to all of the students and parents who asked me to keep writing more books. Thank you to my family for supporting me through every step of this journey.

All rights reserved. No part of this book may be reproduced, transmitted, or stored in an information retrieval system in any form or by any means without prior written permission of the author.

Copyright © 2020

This book was typeset in the following fonts:
Seravek + Mohave + *Heading Pro*

Graphics in Summit Math books are made using the following resources:
Microsoft Excel | Microsoft Word | Desmos | Geogebra | Adobe Illustrator

First printed in 2017

Printed in the U.S.A.

Summit Math Books are written by Alex Joujan.

www.summitmathbooks.com

Learning math through Guided Discovery:
A Guided Discovery learning experience is designed to help you experience a feeling of discovery as you learn each new topic.

Why this curriculum series is named Summit Math:
Learning through Guided Discovery can be compared to climbing a mountain. Climbing and learning both require effort and persistence. In both activities, people naturally move at different paces, but they can reach the summit if they keep moving forward. Whether you race rapidly through these books or step slowly through each scenario, this curriculum is designed to keep advancing your learning until you reach the end of the book.

Guided Discovery Scenarios:
The Guided Discovery Scenarios in this book are written and arranged to show you that new math concepts are related to previous concepts you have already learned. Try to fully understand each scenario before moving on to the next one. To do this, try the scenario on your own first, check your answer when you finish, and then fix any mistakes, if needed. Making mistakes and struggling are essential parts of the learning process.

Homework and Extra Practice Scenarios:
After you complete the scenarios in each Guided Discovery section, you may think you know those topics well, but over time, you will forget what you have learned. Extra practice will help you develop better retention of each topic. Use the Homework and Extra Practice Scenarios to improve your understanding and to increase your ability to retain what you have learned.

The Answer Key:
The Answer Key is included to promote learning. When you finish a scenario, you can get immediate feedback. When the Answer Key is not enough to help you fully understand a scenario, you should try to get additional guidance from another student or a teacher.

Star symbols:
Scenarios marked with a star symbol ★ can be used to provide you with additional challenges. Star scenarios are like detours on a hiking trail. They take more time, but you may enjoy the experience. If you skip scenarios marked with a star, you will still learn the core concepts of the book.

To learn more about Summit Math and to see more resources:
Visit www.summitmathbooks.com.

As you complete scenarios in this part of the book, follow the steps below.

Step 1: Try the scenario.
Read through the scenario on your own or with other classmates. Examine the information carefully. Try to use what you already know to complete the scenario. Be willing to struggle.

Step 2: Check the Answer Key.
When you look at the Answer Key, it will help you see if you fully understand the math concepts involved in that scenario. It may teach you something new. It may show you that you need guidance from someone else.

Step 3: Fix your mistakes, if needed.
If there is something in the scenario that you do not fully understand, do something to help you understand it better. Go back through your work and try to find and fix your errors. Mistakes provide an opportunity to learn. If you need extra guidance, get help from another student or a teacher.

After Step 3, go to the next scenario and repeat this 3-step cycle.

NEED EXTRA HELP?
watch videos online

Teaching videos for every scenario in the Guided Discovery section of this book are available at www.summitmathbooks.com/algebra-2-videos.

CONTENTS

Section 1 **PLOTTING POINTS** 3

Section 2 **SLOPE** 5

Section 3 **SLOPE-INTERCEPT FORM** 9

Section 4 **STANDARD FORM** 17

Section 5 **POINT-SLOPE FORM** 25

Section 6 **AN INTRODUCTION TO TREND LINES** 34

Section 7 **VERTICAL AND HORIZONTAL LINES** 41

Section 8 **LINEAR INEQUALITIES** 45

Section 9 **CUMULATIVE REVIEW** 51

Section 10 **ANSWER KEY** 55

HOMEWORK & EXTRA PRACTICE SCENARIOS 63

Section 1
PLOTTING POINTS

GUIDED DISCOVERY SCENARIOS

At this point, you have already learned how to graph points in the Cartesian Plane. The following scenarios will review this concept to bring your mind back to this topic.

1. Plot each point in the graph. Label each point with its corresponding letter.

    a. (6, 4)   b. (−5, −5)

    c. (−5, 0)   d. (6, −5)

    e. (−5, 4)   f. (0, −5)

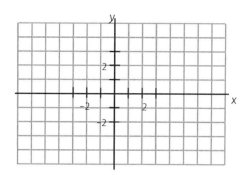

2. Which point is closer to the x-axis?

    Point #1: (77, 57)   Point #2: (78, 56)

3. Plot each point and use estimation to try to guess which point is closest to the location of (0, 0).

    a. (−5, −5)

    b. (5, −5)

    c. (−3, 7)

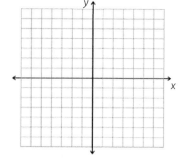

4. The graph shows the value of one share of Sears stock over the course of 6 years. What was the value of Sears stock on the date shown below?

    a. 1/1/2010   b. 1/1/2014

5. Refer to the graph in the previous scenario. On what day was the value of Sears stock the amount shown below?

    a. $30   b. $40

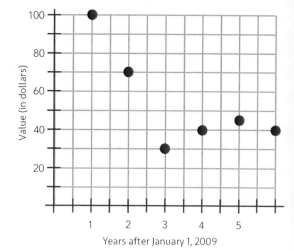

6. In the previous scenario, during which year did the stock price change by...

    a. the greatest amount?   b. the least amount?

Section 2
SLOPE

GUIDED DISCOVERY SCENARIOS

If you plot 2 points and draw a line through them, the slant of the line is called its slope. The slope is a ratio that describes how a line moves up or down as you move along it to the left or right. The following scenarios will review this topic.

7. Determine the slope of the line shown to the right.

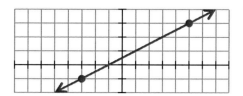

8. Use the graph to determine the slope of each line shown.

a.

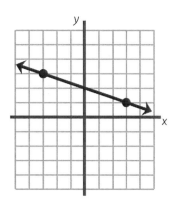

b.

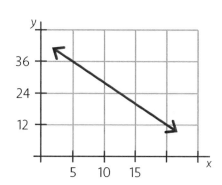

9. Describe the slope of each line using the words positive or negative.

a.

b.

c.

d.

10. Identify the slope of the line shown and explain what the slope means if the graph displays the temperature in the evening.

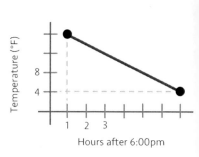

11. Write an expression that shows the slope of the line shown.

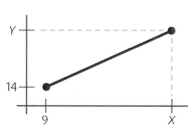

12. Write an expression that shows the slope of the line shown. What is the significance of your answer?

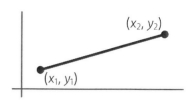

13. A line passes through the points $(11, 17)$ and $(21, 23)$. Without graphing these points, what is the slope of this line?

14. Identify the slope of the line that passes through each pair of points.

   a. $(-13, 5)$ and $(24, 5)$

   b. $(-25, 11)$ and $(-10, 6)$

15. The following table displays points on line L.

   a. What is the slope of line L?

x	2	7	17	M	H
y	-5	-2	4	7	34

   ★b. What is the value of M?

   ★c. What is the value of H?

Use this page to record important ideas in the previous section or for any other writing that helps you learn the topics in this book.

Section 3
SLOPE-INTERCEPT FORM

GUIDED DISCOVERY SCENARIOS

You should already be familiar with linear equations written in Slope-Intercept Form: y = mx + b. In this section, you will review this topic to help you improve your fluency with equations in this form.

16. What is the equation of the line shown in the graph, in Slope-Intercept Form?

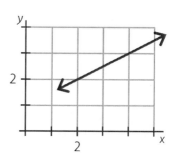

17. Consider the line shown in the graph. Write the equation of this line in Slope-Intercept Form.

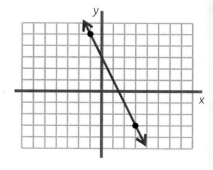

18. If a point is located on a line, it "satisfies" the equation of that line. In the previous scenario, the equation of the line is $y = -2x + 3$.

    a. Does (2, –1) satisfy the equation?   b. Does (–1, 4) satisfy the equation?

19. If an ordered pair satisfies an equation, the equation is true when you replace x and y with the values from that ordered pair. Consider the equation $y = \frac{3}{4}x - 2$.

    a. Does (4, 1) satisfy the equation?   b. Does (–4, –6) satisfy the equation?

20. Identify the exact y-intercept of the line shown.

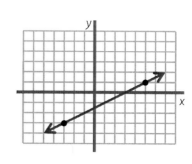

GUIDED DISCOVERY SCENARIOS

21. ★Identify the y-intercept of each line shown.

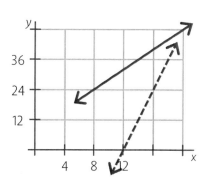

22. The slope of a line is 4. One point on the line is $(-2, 7)$. What is the line's y-intercept?

23. A line's slope is $-\frac{2}{5}$. It passes through the point $(6, 10)$. What is the y-intercept of the line?

24. Consider the ordered pairs $(-5, -2)$ and $(7, -6)$. Determine the equation of the line that passes through the given ordered pairs and then graph the line.

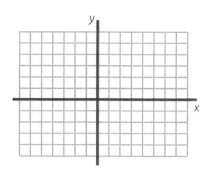

25. Your equation in the previous scenario is written in Slope-Intercept Form: $y = mx + b$. In this form, the equation shows the value of y in terms of x. Consider an equation like $y = x + 7$. Rewrite the equation to show x in terms of y.

26. Several equations are shown below. Fill in the blank to complete each statement.

   a. The equation $F = -3x + 20$ shows _____ in terms of _____.

   b. The equation $R = \dfrac{3-2m}{5}$ shows _____ in terms of _____.

   c. The equation $\pi r^2 = A$ shows _____ in terms of _____.

27. Consider the linear data below:

x	4	8	14	...
H	−1	−7	−16	...

a. Write an equation for H in terms of x

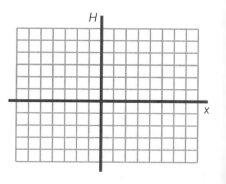

★b. Graph the line.

★c. Is the point (−20, 30) located on the line?

28. Write an equation for C in terms of p.

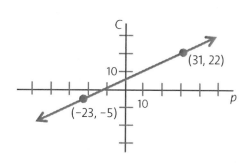

29. Write the equation for the line shown to the right.

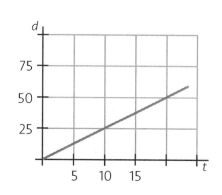

30. A pilot is nearing the end of a flight and at 6:00pm, after flying for several hours at a standard cruising altitude, she starts to descend at a constant rate. At 6:04pm, the plane's altitude is 25,600 feet. At 6:11pm, the plane's altitude is 7,400 feet.

   a. What is the plane's rate of descent?

   b. What was the plane's cruising altitude when the pilot began the descent?

   c. Write a function that relates the altitude A, measured in feet, to the number of minutes m that have passed since the pilot began the descent.

   d. Is it reasonable to use this equation to determine the plane's altitude at 6:15pm?

31. Write the equation for P in terms of r.

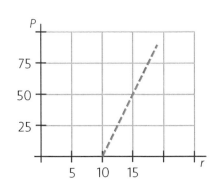

32. Graph all three lines on the same Cartesian Plane.

   a. $y = \dfrac{2}{3}x + 3$ b. $y = \dfrac{2}{3}x - 2$ c. $y = -\dfrac{3}{2}x$

   d. Describe what you notice when you look at the way that these lines appear on the graph.

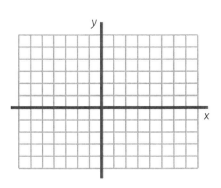

33. In the previous scenario, which two lines are perpendicular and why does this occur?

34. Write the phrase "perpendicular lines have opposite reciprocal slopes" in the space below.

35. Graph the two lines below and pay attention to the result.

   a. Line 1: $y = -\dfrac{2}{3}x$

   b. Line 2: $y = \dfrac{3}{2}x$

   c. What do you notice about the lines?

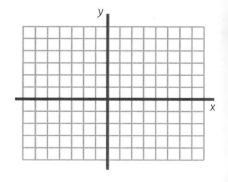

36. ★When divers explore ocean life underwater, they encounter more pressure as they dive deeper. For example, at a depth of 10 feet, the pressure on a diver's body is 19.2 pounds per square inch (psi). At a depth of 18 feet, the pressure is 22.8 pounds per square inch (psi).

   a. If the pressure increases at a constant rate as a diver's depth increases, write a linear function that represents the pressure P in "psi" at a depth of d feet.

   b. What does the P-intercept of this equation represent?

   c. If a diver descends 100 feet, by what amount will the pressure increase?

   d. What is the rate at which the pressure increases as a diver's depth increases? Include the units in your result.

GUIDED DISCOVERY SCENARIOS

37. ★Andre's car has a gas mileage of 33 miles per gallon when he maintains an average speed of 55 miles per hour. Suppose he leaves to go on a road trip with 12 gallons of gas in the car's gas tank, and he maintains an average speed of 55 miles per hour.

    a. How many gallons of gas are in the tank after 3 hours?

    b. Determine the function that models the gallons of gas, G, that remain in his gas tank t hours after he starts driving.

    c. What is the meaning of the G-intercept of this function?

    d. What is the meaning of the t-intercept of this function?

38. Which tables below represent a linear pattern? If the pattern is linear, identify the relationship between x and y for that table.

a.

x	y
1	-3
2	0
3	3
4	6

b.

x	y
1	9
2	8
3	5
4	0

39. ★Do the pairs of x- and y-values in the table follow a linear pattern? If so, write the linear equation that shows the relationship between x and y.

x	y
4	-9
2	-1
1	3
3	-5

NOTES

Use this page to record important ideas in the previous section or for any other writing that helps you learn the topics in this book.

Section 4
STANDARD FORM

GUIDED DISCOVERY SCENARIOS

When a linear equation is in Standard Form, it looks like $Ax + By = C$. To put this simply, the two variables are on the same side of the equation.

40. Consider the equation $6x + 8y = 24$.

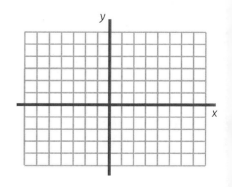

   a. If x is 0, what is the value of y?

   b. If y is 0, what is the value of x?

   c. You can now easily create a graph of this line. Why is this?

   d. Graph the line.

41. Consider the equation $4x - 5y = 20$.

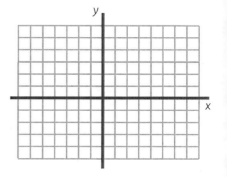

   a. If $x = 0$, what is the value of y?

   b. If $y = 0$, what is the value of x?

   c. Graph the line formed by the equation $4x - 5y = 20$.

   d. Find another ordered pair that satisfies the equation.

42. Consider the equation $-4x - 2y = 10$.

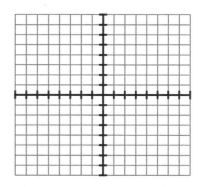

   a. Graph this line by using the strategy of finding the line's x- and y-intercepts. Plot those two points and then draw the line through them.

   b. Using the graph, what is the slope of the line?

43. Circle one of the terms to the right of the statement.

   a. If the coordinates of a point are (___, 0), then it is a(n)   x-intercept   y-intercept

   b. If the coordinates of a point are (0, ___), then it is a(n)   x-intercept   y-intercept

44. Consider the graph shown to the right.

   a. Identify the x-intercept of the line.

   b. Identify the y-intercept of the line.

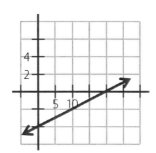

45. Consider the equation $-3x + 4y = 12$.

   a. Identify the x- and y-intercepts of the line formed by this equation.

   b. Display a graph of this equation.

   c. Explain how you could determine if the point $(-3.1, 0.7)$ is located exactly on the line shown.

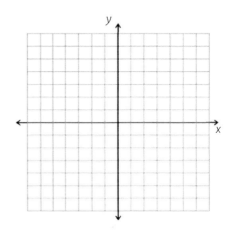

46. ★ Is the point $(-3.1, 0.7)$ located exactly on the line in the previous scenario?

47. ★Draw the following 3 lines on the same graph. Plot ordered pairs that only contain integers.

   a. $6x + 2y = 12$

   b. $0.72x - 2.16y = 4.32$

   c. $-\dfrac{1}{4}x + \dfrac{1}{8}y = \dfrac{1}{2}$

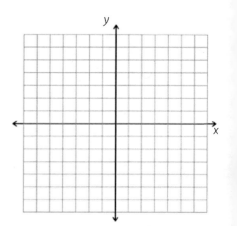

48. ★What shape is formed inside the boundary of the lines in the previous scenario? Be specific.

49. Linear equations can be written in different forms. For example, start with an equation in Slope-Intercept Form, $y = 2x - 9$.

   a. Move the term that contains x to the other side of the equation. Use the space to the right to show your work.

   b. Now arrange the terms to put the "x" term to the left of the "y" term.

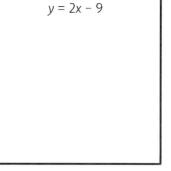

$y = 2x - 9$

After minimal effort, the equation has been converted to Standard Form: $Ax + By = C$.

50. Even if an equation in Slope-Intercept Form contains fractions, it can still be rearranged and written in Standard Form. Consider, for example, the equation $y = -\frac{3}{4}x + \frac{7}{2}$.

$y = -\frac{3}{4}x + \frac{7}{2}$

a. Move the term that contains x to the other side. Use the space to the right to show your work.

b. Write the "x" term to the left of the "y" term.

c. Multiply both sides of the equation by ___. This will clear the fractions to make A, B and C integers.

Now the equation is in Standard Form: Ax + By = C. It is <u>not actually necessary</u> to eliminate the fractions, but the equation looks simpler when A, B, and C are integers.

51. Write each equation in Standard Form, such that A, B and C are integers.

    a. $y = 3x - 2$ b. $y = \frac{2}{5}x + 4$ c. $y = -\frac{1}{3}x - \frac{7}{3}$

52. In these scenarios, it will help if you can change the initial equation somehow.

    a. If $\frac{1}{5}x + \frac{1}{3}y = 2$, what is the value of $3x + 5y$?

    ★b. If $\frac{1}{2}x - \frac{2}{7}y = 1$, what is the value of $8y - 14x$?

GUIDED DISCOVERY SCENARIOS

53. Kiran earns extra money every week by working Fridays and Saturdays. He earns $18 an hour working after school on Fridays, and $24 an hour working on Saturdays.

    a. If he works 4 hours on Friday and y hours on Saturday and he earns a total of $264, what is the value of y?

    b. If he works x hours on Friday and 5 hours on Saturday and he earns a total of $192, what is the value of x?

    c. Kiran works x hours on Friday and y hours on Saturday and he earns $324. Write an equation that relates x and y.

54. In 2015, the toll rate for passing through the Holland Tunnel into New York City was $13 for a car and $22 for a bus. Suppose a total of 3,000 cars and buses pass through the tunnel in one hour, and a total of $46,290 in tolls is collected. There are two equations that relate the number of cars, C, and buses, B, that pass through the tunnel during that hour. Determine these two equations and write them in Standard Form. Do not solve the equations.

55. ★Every year, approximately 34,000,000 vehicles pass through the Holland Tunnel on the way to New York City. Estimate the number of vehicles that pass through the tunnel every hour.

56. A rectangle has a length L and a width W. The perimeter of the rectangle is 22 cm.

    a. Write an equation that relates L and W to the perimeter of the rectangle.

    b. If the length is 5 cm more than the width, what are the dimensions of the rectangle?

57. It is sometimes necessary, or even helpful, to write an equation in a different form. To practice this, rewrite the following equation in Slope-Intercept Form.

$$y - 3 = \frac{1}{2}(x - 8)$$

58. Rewrite the equation $y = \frac{1}{2}x - 1$ in Standard Form. Clear the fractions.

59. Identify the x- and y- intercepts of the line formed by the equation $4x - 7y = 28$.

60. ★The line $Ax + 3.2y = 12$ has an x-intercept at (2.5, 0). What is the value of A?

61. ★What is the y-intercept of the line described in the previous scenario?

62. ★What are the values of A and B if the equation $Ax + By = 1$ has an x-intercept of (4,0) and a y-intercept of (0,5)?

Use this page to record important ideas in the previous section or for any other writing that helps you learn the topics in this book.

Section 5
POINT-SLOPE FORM

GUIDED DISCOVERY SCENARIOS

Now that you have reviewed Slope-Intercept Form and Standard Form, you will learn about a third form for a linear equation. This form is derived from the slope formula.

63. Use what you know about finding the slope of a line to answer each question below.

    a. What is the slope of the line containing the points $(4,7)$ and $(8,5)$?

    b. What is the slope of the line containing the points $(-3, y)$ and $(x, -5)$? You will not be able to simplify the fraction, but write the expression that represents the slope of this line.

    c. What is the slope of the line containing the points (x_1, y_1) and (x_2, y_2)?

64. If you draw a line through two points, (x_1, y_1) and (x_2, y_2), the slope of the line is $m = \dfrac{y_2 - y_1}{x_2 - x_1}$. If you rearrange the formula to isolate $y_2 - y_1$, it will look like $y_2 - y_1 = $ _____. (Fill in the blank.)

65. The previous scenario may be confusing. How can you rearrange the formula $m = \dfrac{y_2 - y_1}{x_2 - x_1}$ to make it look like $y_2 - y_1 = m(x_2 - x_1)$?

66. In the rearranged slope formula, $y_2 - y_1 = m(x_2 - x_1)$, there are 5 variables. Suppose a line has a slope of $\dfrac{1}{3}$ and contains the point $(3, 7)$. If you think of $(3, 7)$ as (x_1, y_1), you can substitute that point and the slope into the rearranged slope formula to obtain $y_2 - \underline{} = \dfrac{1}{3}(x_2 - \underline{})$. (Fill in the blanks.)

GUIDED DISCOVERY SCENARIOS

67. In the formula, $y_2 - 7 = \frac{1}{3}(x_2 - 3)$, the subscripts ($x_2$ and y_2) are only there to distinguish one (x, y) from another (x, y) so the subscripts can be removed, which changes the equation to $y - 7 = \frac{1}{3}(x - 3)$. In the rearranged slope formula, $y_2 - y_1 = m(x_2 - x_1)$, replace the x_2 and y_2 with x and y and write the formula again.

68. The equation $y - 7 = \frac{1}{3}(x - 3)$ forms a line that contains the point (___, ___). This line's slope is ___.

69. Similarly then, the equation $y - 8 = \frac{1}{3}(x - 4)$ forms a line that passes through the point (___, ___).

70. What point is on the line formed by the equation $y + 8 = \frac{1}{3}(x + 4)$?

71. The equation $y - y_1 = m(x - x_1)$ is called the Point-Slope Form for the equation of a line. Why is the name Point-Slope Form assigned to this equation?

72. Given the following information, write the equation of each line in Point-Slope Form.

    a. The point $(3, -5)$ is on the line and the slope of the line is 4.

    b. The point $(-2, 1)$ is on the line and the line's slope is $\frac{1}{2}$.

    c. The line's slope is $-\frac{1}{3}$ and it passes through the point $(-3, 0)$.

GUIDED DISCOVERY SCENARIOS

73. Each of the equations below represents a line. The equations are written in such a way that they show one of the points on the line.

    a. The equation $y-3=2(x-7)$ passes through the point _____.

    b. The equation $y-11=-6(x+12)$ passes through the point _____.

    c. The equation $y+104=4(x+32)$ passes through the point _____.

74. Identify the slope of each line in the previous scenario.

75. Rewrite each of the previous 3 equations in Slope-Intercept Form.

76. The equation $y=mx+b$ is called the Slope-Intercept Form for a line, while the equation $y-y_1=m(x-x_1)$ is called the Point-Slope Form for a line. Why do these equations have different names? What do the names tell you about the lines?

77. Write the equation, in Point-Slope Form, of the line that contains the following points.

    a. $(-1,4)$ and $(5,-8)$ b. $(7,2)$ and $(1,-2)$

78. ★Given Equations 1 and 2 below, which equation represents the line that passes through the points $(-7,-2)$ and $(3,-8)$?

Equation 1: $y+2=\frac{3}{5}(x+7)$ Equation 2: $y-8=-\frac{3}{5}(x-3)$

79. Write the equation of the line shown in Point-Slope Form.

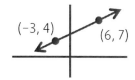

80. Fill in the blanks to complete the equation for each line. Each line is shown below its equation.

a. $y\underline{}=\frac{2}{3}(x\underline{})$

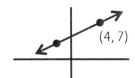

b. $y\underline{}=-\frac{1}{3}(x\underline{})$

81. Without changing the equation, draw the graph for each equation shown below.

a. $y-4=\frac{1}{2}(x-5)$

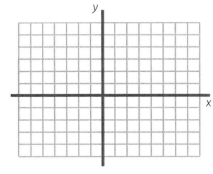

b. $y+3=-(x-2)$

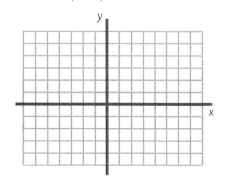

82. Rewrite each of the previous equations in Slope-Intercept Form. Use this rewritten form to confirm that the y-intercept in your equation matches the y-intercept in your graph in the previous scenario.

83. ★One of the three equations below does not belong with the other two. Which one?

   a. $y+7=-(x-15)$ b. $y-12=-(x+4)$ c. $y+14=-(x-8)$

84. ★Graph the previous three equations on the same Cartesian Plane. Label each axis as needed.

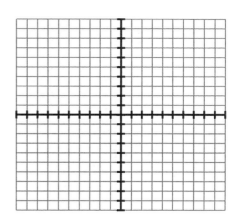

85. Write an equation in Point-Slope Form that shows the relationship between C and p.

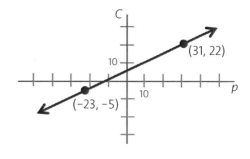

86. Use estimation to analyze the information shown in the graph.

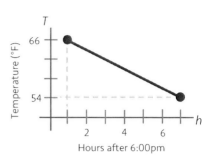

   a. Write an equation for the line in Point-Slope Form.

   b. Write an equation for the line in Slope-Intercept Form.

   c. What is the meaning of the T-intercept of the graph in the context of this scenario?

87. The data in the table below follows a linear relationship.

Hours worked, h	24	40	50	...
Amount paid, P	$276	$460	$575	...

   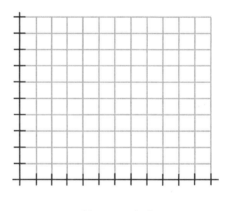

   Hours worked

   a. Write an equation for P in terms of h in Point-Slope Form.

   b. Rewrite the equation in Slope-Intercept Form.

   c. Graph the data in the table in such a way that you clearly display the three data points. Label the coordinates of those three points to make them clearly visible.

   d. How much would you earn if you worked 32.5 hours?

GUIDED DISCOVERY SCENARIOS

88. You have now learned how to write linear equations in 3 different forms, but it is easy to mix these up when you try to remember them. Write the three equation forms below.

    a. Slope-Intercept Form   b. Standard Form   c. Point-Slope Form

89. Without graphing, how can you know that two lines are exactly perpendicular?

90. One line is shown in the graph. Draw a second line that runs perpendicular to the line shown and passes through the point (2, 5).

    a. Write the equation of both lines in Point-Slope Form.

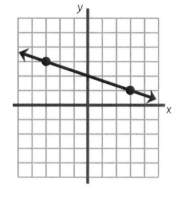

    b. Convert these equations to Slope-Intercept Form.

91. ★Write an equation of a line that is perpendicular to the graph of $-3y+2x=-6$ and has the same y-intercept as the graph of $2x-y=3$. Graph all 3 of the lines to confirm your accuracy.

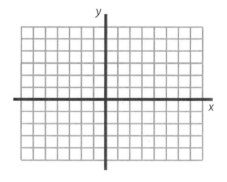

92. Graph the line without changing the equation.

$$y+5=-\frac{1}{4}(x-3)$$

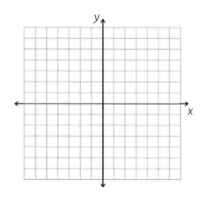

Use this page to record important ideas in the previous section or for any other writing that helps you learn the topics in this book.

Section 6
AN INTRODUCTION TO TREND LINES

GUIDED DISCOVERY SCENARIOS

The next scenarios involve plotting data points. It is convenient when data points line up to a form a straight line, but it is unusual. For example, when you measure the growth of a bamboo plant, during a rainy month there may be more growth, while a dry month may cause less growth. If you look at the growth over several years, though, you may notice a linear trend.

93. A scatter plot is shown in the first graph. The graph below it shows the same scatter plot with a trend line drawn through the points.

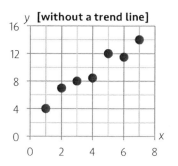

   a. Look at the trend line in the <u>second</u> graph. Which two points would you use to find the equation of the trend line? Why?

   b. What is the equation of the trend line, in Slope-Intercept Form?

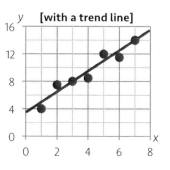

94. Write the equation of the previous trend line in Point-Slope Form.

95. Three scatter plots are shown below. Draw your own trend line through each scatter plot. Your trend line may be different than someone else's trend line. This is an approximation.

a.
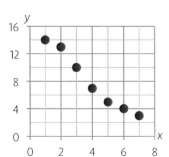

b.
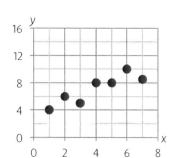

c.
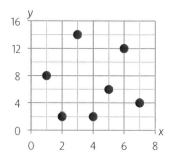

96. Find the slope of each trend line that you drew in the previous scenario.

GUIDED DISCOVERY SCENARIOS

97. Anna saves money every day and she keeps it in a box on her desk. She uses this money when she needs some extra cash to buy something. On May 1st, she has $15 in the box. The table to the right shows the total amount of money in the box at the end of each day between May 1st and May 10th.

Day of the month	Money in the box
1	15
2	20
3	26
4	24
5	34
6	35
7	32
8	36
9	42
10	44

a. Use the data in the table to estimate the average rate at which the amount of money in the box is increasing, in dollars per day.

b. One common mistake students make when calculating the average increase is to find "44 minus 15" and then to divide by 10, since the 10th day is when the box contains $44. Why is it a mistake to divide by 10?

98. The data in the previous table is shown in the two graphs below, with the day of the month marked on the horizontal axis. Which graph has the more accurate trend line? Why?

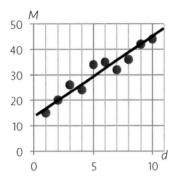 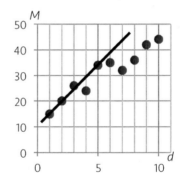

99. Identify the slope of each trend line above.

100. A trend line helps to estimate the amount that the money is increasing by each day. Which trend line in the previous scenario estimates that Anna is setting aside more money every day? Why?

GUIDED DISCOVERY SCENARIOS

101. The chart to the right shows a small data set.

    a. What scenario does this data describe?

    b. Draw an approximate trend line through the scatter plot shown.

    c. Find the equation of your trend line to show the relationship between V, the total view count, and d, the days after the video appears on YouTube.

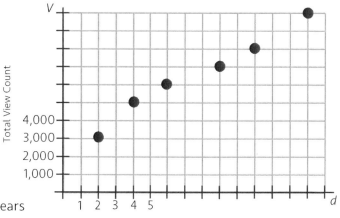

    d. What was the average increase in the views per day over the time period shown?

102. Circle the data sets that show a clear linear trend.

    a. 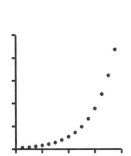   b. 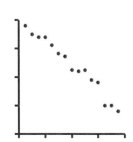   c.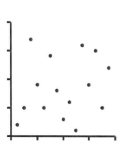

103. The table below shows a selection of world record pole vault heights from 1900 to 1984.

Year	Height (in.)
1912	158
1920	161
1936	174
1942	187
1960	189
1968	213
1976	224
1984	230

    a. Use the data to create a scatter plot.

    b. Draw a line of best fit through the scatter plot.

104. Determine the equation of your trend line in the previous scenario to show the relationship between H and t.

   a. Write the equation in Slope-Intercept Form.

   b. When you write the equation in Slope-Intercept Form, the y-intercept is visible in the equation. In the pole vault scenario, suppose your trend line's y-intercept is $(0, -1919)$. What does this mean in the context of the pole vault scenario?

   c. Since the y-intercept is not useful information in the pole-vault scenario, you can write the equation in a different form. What form of a linear equation would be more useful and easier to write in the pole-vault scenario?

105. Use Point-Slope Form to write the equation of your trend line in the previous scenario.

106. Use your previous equation to answer the following questions.

   a. What was the average increase of the pole vault record, in inches per year?

   b. The world record in 2010 was 241 inches. Does your equation predict this?

   c. Can you rely on your equation to predict the record in 2030?

107. ★The graph shows how the value of Sears stock changed over a specific time period.

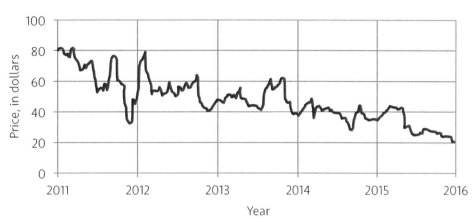

a. Estimate the rate at which the value of Sears stock is decreasing each year during the time period shown in the graph.

b. Estimate the month and year that Sears stock price will lose all of its value.

108. The graph shows the number of annual vacation days for people who have worked at a company for a certain numbers of years.

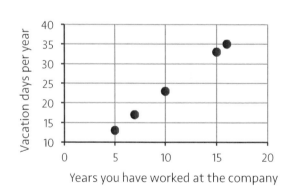

a. If you have worked at the company for 12 years, how many vacation days do you get that year?

b. How many vacation days are given to someone who has worked at the company 30 years?

c. When new employees join the company, how many vacation days do they start out with?

Use this page to record important ideas in the previous section or for any other writing that helps you learn the topics in this book.

Section 7
VERTICAL AND HORIZONTAL LINES

109. Select two ordered pairs from the line shown and find the slope of this line. What do you notice?

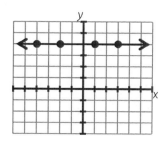

110. Select two ordered pairs from the line shown and find the slope of this line. What do you notice?

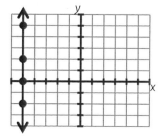

111. What is the slope of a horizontal line? Explain why a horizontal line has this particular slope.

112. What is the slope of a vertical line? Explain why a vertical line has this particular slope.

113. Plot a point that has a *y*-value of 4. Now plot another point that has a *y*-value of 4. Pick three more points such that each has a *y*-value of 4. Draw a line that passes through all of your points. What do you notice about your line? Try to figure out the equation of this line.

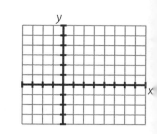

114. Plot a point that has an *x*-value of −5. Now plot another point that has an *x*-value of −5. Pick three more points such that each has an *x*-value of −5. Draw a line that passes through all of your points. What do you notice about your line? Try to figure out the equation of this line.

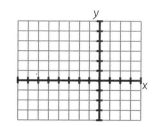

115. Two lines are shown on the Cartesian Plane to the right.

   a. Identify the equation of the dashed line.

   b. Identify the equation of the solid line.

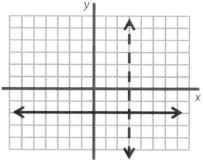

116. Identify the rate shown in the graph and explain what it means in the context of the scenario.

117. Identify the rate shown in the graph and explain what it means in the context of the scenario.

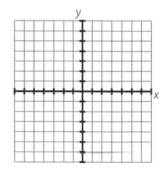

118. Graph the lines shown below on the same Cartesian Plane.

   a. $y - 5 = -(x + 4)$

   b. $y + 2 = 6$

   c. $y + 3 = 8 - (x - y)$

119. Calculate the area of the region bordered by the three lines in the previous scenario.

NOTES

Use this page to record important ideas in the previous section or for any other writing that helps you learn the topics in this book.

Section 8
LINEAR INEQUALITIES

GUIDED DISCOVERY SCENARIOS

120. In the Cartesian plane, plot all of the ordered pairs that have an *x*-value of 3.

    a. How many points can you find?

    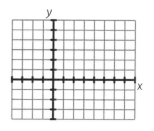

    b. In the same plane to the right, graph all of the ordered pairs that have an *x*-value that is less than 3. How many points can you find?

When you combine the points that lie along the vertical line in your graph above with the points that occupy the space to the left of the vertical line, these points form the solution of the inequality $x \leq 3$.

121. In the graph shown, plot all of the points that form the solution to the inequality $x \geq 3$.

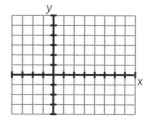

122. In the Cartesian plane shown, plot every ordered pair with a *y*-value of −2.

    a. How many points can you find?

    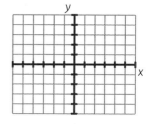

    b. In the same plane, graph all of the ordered pairs that have a *y*-value that is <u>greater</u> than −2. How many points can you find?

When you combine the points that lie along the line in your graph above with the points that occupy the space above the line, these points form the solution of the inequality $y \geq -2$.

123. Plot all of the points that form the solution to the inequality $y \leq -2$.

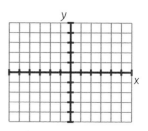

124. How could you change your graph in the previous scenario to display the solution region for the inequality $y < -2$?

125. Graph the given inequality.

   a. $x > -4$

   b. $y > 1$

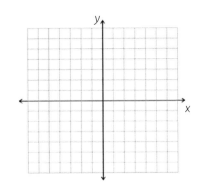
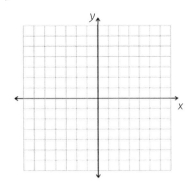

126. Write the inequality that has the solution set shown in each graph below.

   a.
   b.
   c.

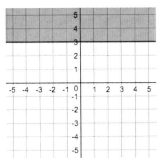
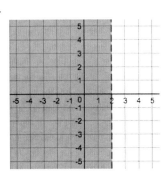
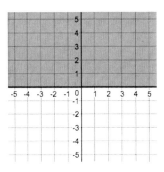

127. Rule A states that you may only plot a point if its *y*-value is exactly the same as its *x*-value.

   a. On the graph shown, plot 3 points that follow Rule A.

   b. On the same graph, quickly plot one hundred more points that follow Rule A.

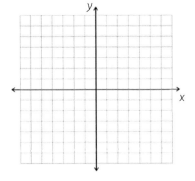

128. If you plot them correctly, the points that satisfy Rule A form a single line. The equation for that line is quite simple: $y = x$. Now consider Rule B. Rule B states that you may only plot a point if it has a *y*-value that is less than its *x*-value. For example, (5, 3) does follow the rule because the *y*-value (3) is less than the *x*-value (5).

   a. Write down five more points that follow Rule B. Try to create a wide variety of numbers in your coordinates.

   b. Plot your five points in the graph shown.

   c. Quickly plot one hundred more points that follow Rule B.

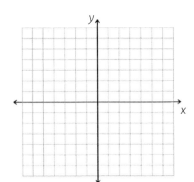

GUIDED DISCOVERY SCENARIOS

If you plot them correctly, the points that satisfy Rule B in the previous scenario fill in all of the space below the line $y=x$. The points on the line are NOT part of the solution. This can be shown by drawing the line as a dashed line. The shaded region (the points that satisfy Rule B) represents the solution to the inequality $y<x$.

129. Part of an inequality is shown below. The boundary line for the inequality is also shown. State which side of the line you would shade to finish the graph of the inequality.

   a. $y > \underline{\qquad}$ b. $y \leq \underline{\qquad}$ c. $x < \underline{\qquad}$

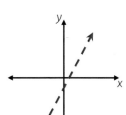
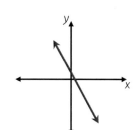
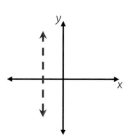

130. Use the word <u>positive</u> or <u>negative</u> to describe the slope of each line shown in the previous scenario.

131. In each of the graphs below, try to plot the solution region for the inequality shown.

   a. $y > x + 3$
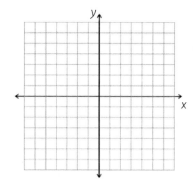

   b. $y \geq \dfrac{1}{2}x - 3$
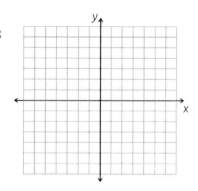

132. Write the inequality that has the solution set shown in each graph below.

   a.
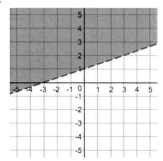

   b.
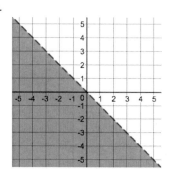

   c.
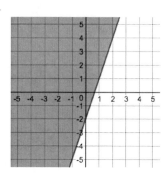

133. Is the point (0,0) located in the solution region for any of the inequalities in the previous scenario?

134. Is the ordered pair (0,0) located in the solution region for each of the inequalities shown below?

   a. $y \geq 5x$

   b. $y > -2x - 3$

   c. $-7x + 11y < -1$

135. Graph each inequality below.

   a. $x + y < 4$

   b. $3x - 4y \leq 12$

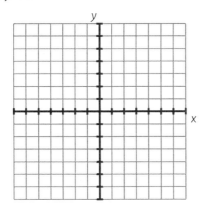
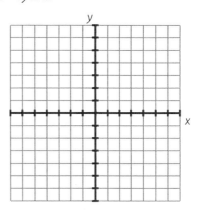

136. Graph each inequality below.

   a. $x > -3$

   b. $y \leq \dfrac{5}{2}$

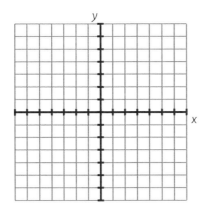
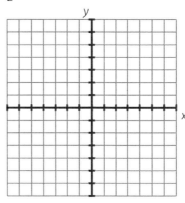

NOTES

Use this page to record important ideas in the previous section or for any other writing that helps you learn the topics in this book.

Section 9
CUMULATIVE REVIEW

137. A linear function is defined by the equation $f(x) = 4x - 8$.

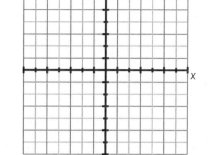

a. What is the value of $f(4)$?

b. What is the value of $f(0)$?

c. If you know the answers to the previous two questions, how does this help you plot points on the linear function?

d. Graph the function in the plane shown. Do not change the scale of either axis. Make each grid line represent a width of 1 unit.

138. Without using a calculator, which expression has a greater value? Explain your reasoning.

Expression 1: $\left(\dfrac{11}{9} - \dfrac{1}{3}\right)^2$ Expression 2: $\left(\dfrac{11}{15} + \dfrac{1}{3}\right)^2$

139. Three kids (X, Y and Z) leave school at the same time and walk home.

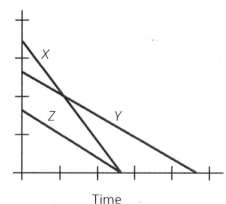

a. Who walked the slowest? How do you know?

b. Whose house is closest to the school? How do you know?

c. Who arrived at home first?

GUIDED DISCOVERY SCENARIOS

140. In the graph to the right, imagine that you can lift the line off of the page and move it around. If you slide the line up 1 unit and to the right 3 units, what is the slope of the line after you have moved it?

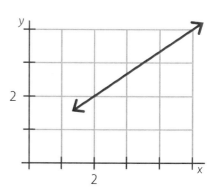

141. Consider the function, $C(n)$, shown in the graph.

    a. What is the value of $C(2)$?

    b. What is the value of n if $C(n)=1$?

    c. Identify the domain of the function.

    d. Identify the range of the function.

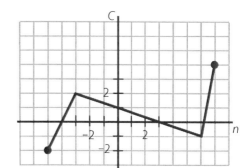

142. Identify the interval(s) on which the previous function is increasing.

143. The graph in the previous scenario is formed by taking segments from 3 different lines. Write the equation for each of the 3 lines.

144. If you graphed each of the 3 lines that you identified in the previous scenario, the lines would extend in both directions without ending. In the previous scenario, however, only a small portion of each line is shown because they have restricted domains. Identify the restricted domain for each line.

    a. The restricted domain for the line given by the equation $C = 2n + 8$ is ____ $\leq n \leq$ ____ .

    b. The restricted domain for the line $C = -\frac{1}{3}n + 1$ is _____ .

    c. The restricted domain for the line $C = 5n - 31$ is _____ .

NOTES

Use this page to record important ideas in the previous section or for any other writing that helps you learn the topics in this book.

Section 10
ANSWER KEY

1.	(graph with plotted points)
2.	Point #2 (the point with the smaller y-value is closer to the x-axis)
3.	The points (–5, –5) and (5, –5) are both the same distance from (0, 0) and they are both closer than (–3, 7).
4.	a. $100 b. $45
5.	a. 1/1/12 b. 1/1/13 and 1/1/15
6.	a. 2011 b. 2013 and 2014
7.	$\frac{1}{2}$
8.	a. $-\frac{1}{3}$ b. $-\frac{24}{15} \to -\frac{8}{5}$
9.	a. positive b. negative c. negative d. neither (the slope is 0)
10.	Slope is –2 → the temperature is decreasing 2 degrees per hour.
11.	$\frac{Y-14}{X-9}$ or $\frac{14-Y}{9-X}$
12.	$\frac{y_2-y_1}{x_2-x_1}$ or $\frac{y_1-y_2}{x_1-x_2}$. This ratio is the typical structure of the slope formula.
13.	slope $= \frac{23-17}{21-11} = \frac{6}{10} = \frac{3}{5}$
14.	a. slope $= \frac{5-5}{24-(-13)} = \frac{0}{37} = 0$ b. slope $= \frac{6-11}{-10-(-25)} = \frac{-5}{15} = -\frac{1}{3}$
15.	a. $\frac{3}{5}$ b. 22 c. 67
16.	$y=\frac{1}{2}x+1$
17.	$y=-2x+3$
18.	a. Yes, it is on the line. b. No, it is not on the line.
19.	a. Yes. $1=\frac{3}{4}(4)-2 \to 1=3-2 \to 1=1$ b. No. $-6=\frac{3}{4}(-4)-2 \to -6 \neq -5$
20.	$(0,-1.5)$
21.	Solid line: (0, 8) Dashed line: (0, –72)
22.	$(0,15)$ $y=4x+b \to 7=4(-2)+b \to b=15$
23.	$(0,12.4)$ or $\left(0,12\frac{2}{5}\right)$ $y=-\frac{2}{5}x+b \to 10=-\frac{2}{5}(6)+b \to b=12\frac{2}{5}$
24.	$y=-\frac{1}{3}x-\frac{11}{3}$
25.	$x=y-7$
26.	a. F in terms of x b. R in terms of m c. A in terms of r
27.	a. $H=-\frac{3}{2}x+5$ b. (graph) c. No, plug in (–20, 30) → $30 \neq -\frac{3}{2}(20)+5$
28.	$C=\frac{1}{2}p+6.5$
29.	$d=2.5t$
30.	Two points: (4, 25,600) and (11, 7,400) a. 2,600 feet per minute b. 36,000 ft c. $A=36,000-2,600m$ d. No. At 6:15pm, plane would have an altitude of –3,000 ft.
31.	$P = 10r - 100$

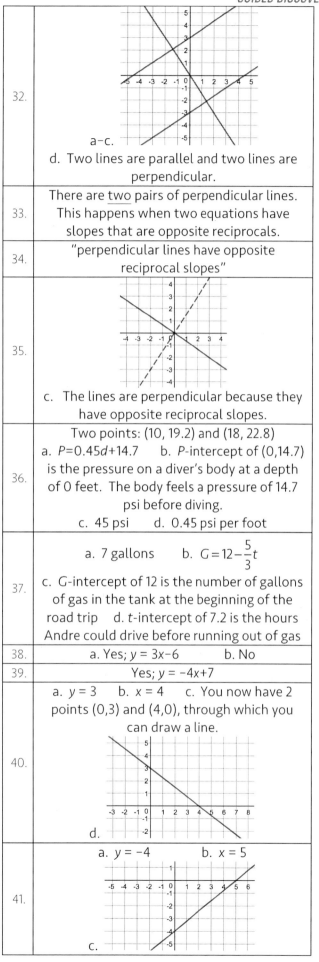

32.	a–c. d. Two lines are parallel and two lines are perpendicular.
33.	There are <u>two</u> pairs of perpendicular lines. This happens when two equations have slopes that are opposite reciprocals.
34.	"perpendicular lines have opposite reciprocal slopes"
35.	c. The lines are perpendicular because they have opposite reciprocal slopes.
36.	Two points: (10, 19.2) and (18, 22.8) a. $P=0.45d+14.7$ b. P-intercept of $(0,14.7)$ is the pressure on a diver's body at a depth of 0 feet. The body feels a pressure of 14.7 psi before diving. c. 45 psi d. 0.45 psi per foot
37.	a. 7 gallons b. $G=12-\dfrac{5}{3}t$ c. G-intercept of 12 is the number of gallons of gas in the tank at the beginning of the road trip d. t-intercept of 7.2 is the hours Andre could drive before running out of gas
38.	a. Yes; $y = 3x-6$ b. No
39.	Yes; $y = -4x+7$
40.	a. $y = 3$ b. $x = 4$ c. You now have 2 points (0,3) and (4,0), through which you can draw a line. d.
41.	a. $y = -4$ b. $x = 5$ c.

42.	d. Many possible points. The extra point should be on the line when you graph it. a. b. $\dfrac{-2}{1}$ or -2
43.	a. x-intercept b. y-intercept
44.	a. (20, 0) b. (0, −4)
45.	a. x-int: (−4, 0) y-int: (0, 3) b. c. Replace x with −3.1 and y with 0.7. If the equation is true, then the point is on the line.
46.	No. $-3(-3.1) + 4(0.7) = 12.1$ (If the point was on the line, the left side of the equation would equal 12)
47.	a, b, c.
48.	Right triangle (2 of the lines are perpendicular because their slopes are opposite reciprocals)
49.	a. $y-2x=-9$ b. $-2x+y=-9$
50.	a. $y+\dfrac{3}{4}x=\dfrac{7}{2}$ b. $\dfrac{3}{4}x+y=\dfrac{7}{2}$ c. Multiply by 4. $3x + 4y = 14$
51.	a. $-3x+y=-2$ b. $-2x+5y=20$ c. $x+3y=-7$
52.	a. multiply both sides by 15 → $3x+5y=30$ b. multiply both sides by −28 → $8y-14x=-28$
53.	a. $y=8$ b. $x=4$ c. $18x+24y=324$
54.	$C + B = 3{,}000$ and $13C + 22B = 46{,}290$
55.	Divide by 365, then 24 → 3,881 cars/hr
56.	a. $2L + 2W = 22$ b. $2(W+5)+2W = 22$; $L = 8$ cm, $W = 3$ cm
57.	a. $y=\dfrac{1}{2}x-1$
58.	$-x + 2y = -2$ or $x - 2y = 2$
59.	x-int: (7, 0) y-int: (0, −4)

#	
60.	A = 4.8
61.	(0, 3.75)
62.	$A = \frac{1}{4}$ $B = \frac{1}{5}$
63.	a. $\frac{5-7}{8-4}$ or $\frac{7-5}{4-8} \to -\frac{1}{2}$ b. $\frac{-5-y}{x+3}$ or $\frac{y+5}{-3-x}$ c. $\frac{y_2-y_1}{x_2-x_1}$ or $\frac{y_1-y_2}{x_1-x_2}$
64.	$y_2 - y_1 = m(x_2 - x_1)$
65.	Clear the fraction by multiplying both sides of the equation by the expression $x_2 - x_1$.
66.	$y_2 - 7 = \frac{1}{3}(x_2 - 3)$
67.	$y - y_1 = m(x - x_1)$
68.	point: (3, 7) slope: $\frac{1}{3}$
69.	point: (4, 8)
70.	(−4, −8) To see why the numbers are negative, remember that subtracting a negative number can be written as addition: $y-(-8)=\frac{1}{3}[x-(-4)] \to y+8=\frac{1}{3}(x+4)$
71.	This equation shows a <u>point</u> on the line and the <u>slope</u> of that line.
72.	a. $y+5=4(x-3)$ b. $y-1=\frac{1}{2}(x+2)$ c. $y=-\frac{1}{3}(x+3)$
73.	a. $(7,3)$ b. $(-12,11)$ c. $(-32,-104)$
74.	a. 2 b. −6 c. 4
75.	a. $y-3=2x-14 \to y=2x-11$ b. $y-11=-6x-72 \to y=-6x-61$ c. $y+104=4x+128 \to y=4x+24$
76.	The Slope-Intercept Form shows you the slope and the y-intercept of the line that it describes, while the Point-Slope Form shows you the slope and a point on the line (but not typically the y-intercept).
77.	a. $y-4=-2(x+1)$ or $y+8=-2(x-5)$ b. $y-2=\frac{2}{3}(x-7)$ or $y+2=\frac{2}{3}(x-1)$
78.	Neither equation is correct. Equation 1 has an incorrect slope and Equation 2 should have y + 8 instead of y − 8.
79.	$y-4=\frac{1}{3}(x+3)$ or $y-7=\frac{1}{3}(x-6)$

#	
80.	a. $y-7=\frac{2}{3}(x-4)$ b. $y-4=-\frac{1}{3}(x+5)$
81.	a. 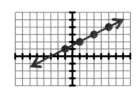 b. 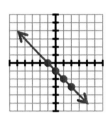
82.	a. $y=\frac{1}{2}x+\frac{3}{2}$ b. $y=-x-1$
83.	Two of the equations represent the same line, but the equation in part c does not.
84.	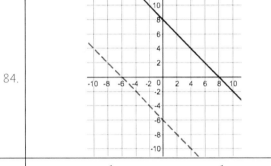
85.	$C-22=\frac{1}{2}(p-31)$ or $C+5=\frac{1}{2}(p+23)$
86.	a. $T-66=-2(h-1)$ or $T-54=-2(h-7)$ b. $T=-2h+68$ c. The T-intercept is the temperature at 6pm.
87.	a. $P-276=11.5(h-24)$ b. $P=11.5h$ c. 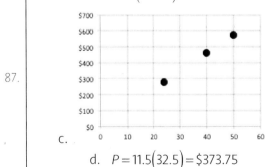 d. $P=11.5(32.5)=\$373.75$
88.	a. $y = mx + b$ b. $Ax + By = C$ c. $y-y_1=m(x-x_1)$
89.	The slopes must be opposite reciprocals.
90.	a. original line: $y-1=-\frac{1}{3}(x-3)$ or

91.	$y-2=-\frac{1}{3}(x-0)$ or $y-3=-\frac{1}{3}(x+3)$ etc... drawn line: $y-5=3(x-2)$ or $y-2=3(x-1)$ or $y+1=3(x-0)$ etc... b. original: $y=-\frac{1}{3}x+2$; drawn: $y=3x-1$	99.	line because it shows the trend of the entire group of points, with some points above the line and others below the line. [Left] points on the line: (2, 20) and (9, 42) Approx. slope: $3\frac{1}{7}$ [Right] points on the line: (1, 15) and (5, 34) Approx. slope: $4\frac{3}{4}$
91.	[graph with lines intersecting] $y=-\frac{3}{2}x-3$	100.	The line on the right; the slope is steeper
92.	[graph showing line through (3, -5)]	101.	a. The total view count of a video after it has been posted on YouTube [scatter plot with trend line] b. c. points: (2, 3000) and (14, 10000); approx. equation: $V=583d+1833$ d. ≈583
93.	a. (3, 8) and (7, 14); The trend line passes exactly through these points. b. $y = 1.5x + 3.5$	102.	Circle the data set in part b.
94.	$y-8=1.5(x-3)$ or $y-14=1.5(x-7)$	103.	[scatter plot with trend line] a and b.
95.	a. [scatter plot with decreasing trend line] b. [scatter plot with increasing trend line] c. no trend line needed because the points do not form a linear pattern	104.	points: (1920, 161) and (1968, 213) a. equation: $H=1\frac{1}{12}t-1919$ b. It means the pole vault record was −1919 inches in the year 0. This is not a meaningful piece of information. c. Point-Slope Form
96.	a. slope is close to −2 b. slope is close to 1 c. slope cannot be calculated because there is no trend line	105.	If you use the points (1920, 161) and (1968, 213) then your equation could be $H-161=1\frac{1}{12}(t-1920)$ or $H-213=1\frac{1}{12}(t-1968)$
97.	a. approx. $3 per day b. From day 1 to day 10, there are only 9 times that the amount of money changes so you would need to divide by 9	106.	a. ≈1 in./yr b. $H-161=1\frac{1}{12}(2010-1920) \rightarrow H=258.5$ The equation predicts a much higher record. c. No, the equation is only helpful if the data continues to follow a linear trend.
98.	The left graph has a more accurate trend	107.	a. possible points on a trend line: (2011, 80), (2016, 20) = $\frac{\$60}{5 \text{ years}}$ → approx. $12/yr b. approx. Sept. 1, 2017 (two-thirds of the way into 2017)
		108.	Draw a trend line. The slope of the trend

	line is 2 days per year. The y-intercept of the line is 3 days. a. 27 days b. 63 days c. 3 days
109.	The slope is 0
110.	The slope is undefined
111.	A horizontal line has a slope of 0, because it does not "rise." A fraction of $\frac{0}{\text{nonzero}}$ has a value of 0.
112.	A vertical line has an undefined slope, because it does not "run." A fraction of $\frac{\text{nonzero}}{0}$ is undefined.
113.	Equation: y = 4
114.	Equation: x = -5
115.	a. x = 3 b. y = -2
116.	The dollars earned does not increase so the rate is $0 per additional hour worked.
117.	The rate is undefined.
118.	
119.	Area = $\frac{1}{2}(8)(8)$ = 32 units^2
120.	a. infinitely many points b. infinitely many points
121.	
122.	a. infinitely many points b. infinitely many points
123.	
124.	Draw a dashed boundary line to show that the points on that line are NOT part of the solution region
125.	a. b.
126.	a. $y \geq 3$ b. $x < 2$ c. $y \geq 0$
127.	b.
128.	c.
129.	a. above the line b. below c. to the left
130.	a. positive b. negative c. neither (it is undefined)

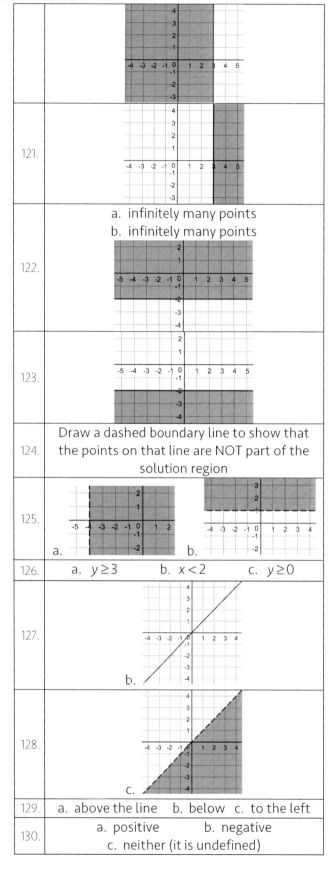

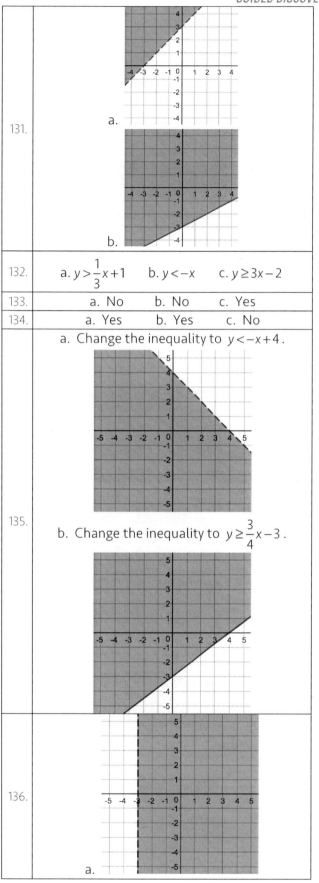

132.	a. $y > \frac{1}{3}x + 1$ b. $y < -x$ c. $y \geq 3x - 2$
133.	a. No b. No c. Yes
134.	a. Yes b. Yes c. No
138.	Expression 1 has a value less than 1 while Expression 2 is greater than 1. Thus, Expression 2 is greater.
139.	a. Y; line has the most gradual slope b. Z; smallest initial distance from home c. X and Z arrived at same time
140.	The slope will still be $\frac{2}{3}$.
141.	a. $\frac{1}{3}$ b. $n = -3.5, 0, 6.4$ c. $-5 \leq n \leq 7$ d. $-2 \leq C \leq 4$
142.	$-5 < n < -3$ and $6 < n < 7$
143.	$C = 2n + 8$; $C = -\frac{1}{3}n + 1$; $C = 5n - 31$
144.	a. $-5 \leq n \leq -3$ b. $-3 \leq n \leq 6$ c. $6 \leq n \leq 7$

Item 136 (partial answer visible): a.

Item 137 answers: a. $f(4) = 8$ b. $f(0) = -8$ c. you now have 2 points on the linear function: (4, 8) and (0, -8)

HOMEWORK & EXTRA PRACTICE SCENARIOS

As you complete scenarios in this part of the book, you will practice what you learned in the guided discovery sections. You will develop a greater proficiency with the vocabulary, symbols and concepts presented in this book. Practice will improve your ability to retain these ideas and skills over longer periods of time.

There is an Answer Key at the end of this part of the book. Check the Answer Key after every scenario to ensure that you are accurately practicing what you have learned. If you struggle to complete any scenarios, try to find someone who can guide you through them.

CONTENTS

Section 1 **REVIEW** 65

Section 2 **PLOTTING POINTS** 67

Section 3 **SLOPE** 69

Section 4 **SLOPE-INTERCEPT FORM** 73

Section 5 **STANDARD FORM** 79

Section 6 **POINT-SLOPE FORM** 84

Section 7 **AN INTRODUCTION TO TREND LINES** 90

Section 8 **VERTICAL AND HORIZONTAL LINES** 96

Section 9 **LINEAR INEQUALITIES** 99

Section 10 **CUMULATIVE REVIEW** 104

Section 11 **ANSWER KEY** 107

Section 1
REVIEW

HOMEWORK & EXTRA PRACTICE SCENARIOS

To solve an equation, you "undo" operations one at a time to isolate a specific variable. The equations that follow are arranged in a specific order to lead you through progressively more difficult equations.

1. Solve each equation by undoing operations until you isolate the given variable. Show your work as you perform each operation.

    a. $1.5x = 18$
    b. $x - 1.5 = 18$
    c. $\dfrac{x}{1.5} = 18$

2. Solve each equation by undoing operations until you isolate the given variable. Show your work as you perform each operation.

    a. $\dfrac{3}{2}x = 18$
    b. $1.5x + 3.5 = 21.5$
    c. $1.5x - 6.5 = 3x - 24.5$

3. Each equation below contains terms with fractions. To make equations like this easier to solve, it is useful to clear the fractions by multiplying both sides by a single number. In each equation below, write the number you would multiply by to clear the fractions. Do <u>not</u> solve the equation.

    a. $\dfrac{1}{3}x - 5 = \dfrac{13}{3}$
    b. $\dfrac{5x}{8} - \dfrac{7}{4} = \dfrac{5}{2}$
    c. $\dfrac{3}{10}x - \dfrac{6}{5} = \dfrac{3}{4}x + \dfrac{3}{2}$

4. In each equation in the previous scenario, clear the fractions and write the resulting equation. Do <u>not</u> solve the resulting equation.

5. Isolate the variable "y" in each equation.

    a. $-2x + 3y = 6$
    b. $3.6x + 2.4y = 7.2$

6. Isolate y in the equation $\dfrac{1}{12}x + \dfrac{1}{4}y = -\dfrac{1}{4}$.

Section 2
PLOTTING POINTS

HOMEWORK & EXTRA PRACTICE SCENARIOS

At this point, you have already learned how to graph points in the Cartesian Plane. The following scenarios will review these concepts to bring your mind back to this topic.

7. Write the coordinates of each point shown in the Cartesian Plane.

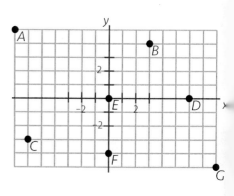

8. Which point is closer to the y-axis?

   Point #1: (–13, 51)   Point #2: (–12, 52)

9. Plot each point and use estimation to try to guess which point is closest to the location of (0, 0).

   a. (–3, 4)

   b. (4, 3)

   c. (0, –5)

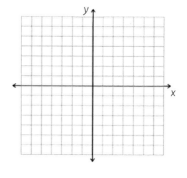

10. The graph to the right shows the monthly sales for a fireworks store. What were the total sales in each month shown?

    a. July   b. September

11. Refer to the graph in the previous scenario. In what month did the sales total the amount shown?

    c. $200,000   b. $150,000

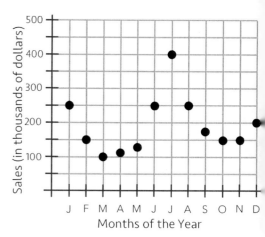

12. In the previous scenario, between which two consecutive months did sales change by...

    a. the smallest amount?   b. the largest amount?

Section 3
SLOPE

If you plot 2 points and draw a line through them, the slant of the line is called its slope. The slope is a ratio that describes how the line moves up or down as you move along it to the left or right.

13. Describe the slope of each line using the words positive or negative.

a.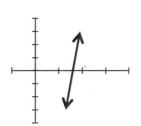

b.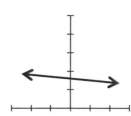

c.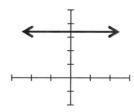

14. Determine the slope of each line shown.

a.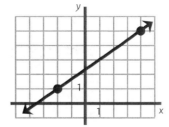

b.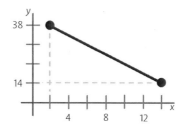

15. Three turtles are entered into a race at the county festival. The graph shown displays the results for the entire race.

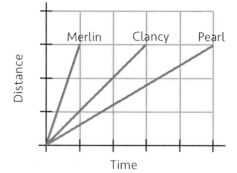

a. Which turtle had the slowest walking speed?

b. How did you make your previous choice?

★c. If each horizontal axis mark represents 30 seconds and each vertical axis mark represents 4 meters, how fast did Pearl walk, in meters per second?

16. The graphs below show the paycheck totals for two lifeguards based on their total hours worked during the week.

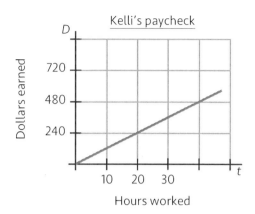
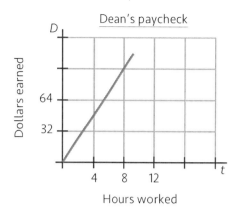

a. Which lifeguard earns more money per hour, Kelli or Dean?

b. How much do they each earn per hour?

17. Write an expression that represents the slope of the line shown.

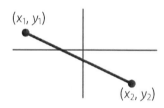

18. A line passes through the points (−10, 4) and (6, 24). Without graphing these points, what is the slope of this line?

19. Identify the slope of the line that passes through each pair of points.

a. $(5, -12)$ and $(-10, 3)$

b. $(101, -3)$ and $(101, 8)$

20. The table displays four of the points on line A.

    a. What is the slope of line A?

x	20	14	11	E
y	−10	−2	2	18

    b. What is the value of E?

21. Determine the value of K that would make the two lines parallel.

    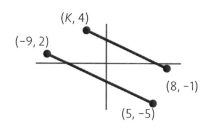

22. What is the slope of the line represented by the equation below?

    $2y = 5x + 10$

23. What is the slope of the line represented by the equation below?

    $3x - 10y = 40$

Section 4
SLOPE-INTERCEPT FORM

HOMEWORK & EXTRA PRACTICE SCENARIOS

24. When a linear equation is written in Slope-Intercept Form, what is its structure?

25. Consider the line shown in the graph. Write the equation of this line in Slope-Intercept Form.

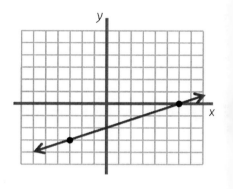

26. If a point is located on a line, it "satisfies" the equation of that line.

    a. Does the point (3, −1) satisfy the equation in the previous scenario?

    b. Does the point (−9, −4) satisfy the equation in the previous scenario?

27. How can you determine if the ordered pair (−15, −13) satisfies the equation $y = \frac{4}{5}x - 1$?

28. Write the equation of the line in Slope-Intercept Form.

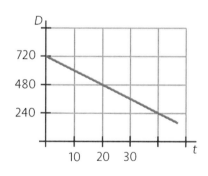

29. Graph the line given by the equation $9x + 9y = 45$.

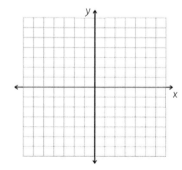

HOMEWORK & EXTRA PRACTICE SCENARIOS

30. Graph both lines on the same Cartesian Plane.

   a. $y = -\dfrac{5}{4}x + 1$ b. $y = \dfrac{4}{5}x - 1$

   c. Describe what you notice when you look at the way that these lines appear on the graph.

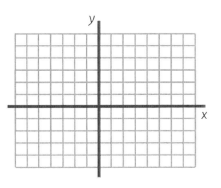

31. The slope of a line is 7. One point on the line is $(-2, 11)$. What is the line's y-intercept?

32. A line has a slope of $\dfrac{5}{6}$, and it passes through the point $(12, -7)$. What are the coordinates of the line's y-intercept?

33. Identify the y-intercept of each line shown.

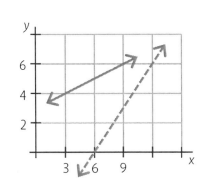

34. Identify the equation, in Slope-Intercept Form, for each line in the previous scenario.

35. Consider the ordered pairs (6, –1) and (–3, 5). Determine the equation of the line that passes through the given ordered pairs and then graph the line to confirm that your equation is accurate.

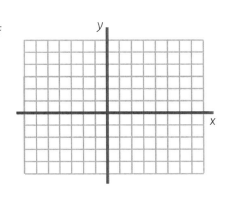

36. Your equation in the previous scenario is written in the form $y = mx + b$. In this form, the equation shows the value of y in terms of x. Consider an equation like $y = 3x - 12$. Rewrite the equation to show x in terms of y.

37. Write an equation for M in terms of t, in Slope-Intercept Form.

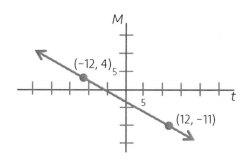

38. Consider the linear data below:

f	−20	−5	15	...
C	−7	−4	0	...

a. Write an equation for C in terms of f and graph the line.

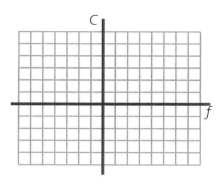

b. Is the point (40, −5) located on the line?

39. Determine the equations of each line shown to the right.

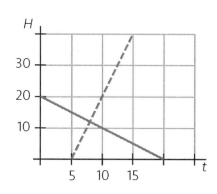

HOMEWORK & EXTRA PRACTICE SCENARIOS

40. A candle is lit at night and it continues to burn until it disappears. The graph shows the weight of the candle over a small period of time.

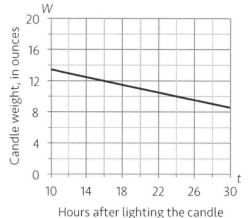

   a. How fast is the candle's weight decreasing, in ounces per hour?

   b. What was the candle's weight 6 hours after it was initially lit?

   c. How many hours will the candle burn before it disappears?

41. For the previous scenario, write an expression that shows the candle's weight after it has been burning for H hours.

42. When the new World Trade Center skyscraper opened, its elevators were among the world's fastest. If you ride to the top floor without stopping, the elevator gradually accelerates at first and then it maintains a constant speed until it nears the end of the ride. After riding for 20 seconds, you will already be 600 feet above the ground, and your height will increase to 1,095 feet above the ground after you have been riding for 35 seconds.

   a. How fast does the elevator rise, measured in feet per second?

   ★b. Convert your speed measurement to miles per hour.

   c. What is your height after you have been riding for 30 seconds?

43. Consider two lines, Line 1 and Line 2. The equation for Line 1 is $y=-\frac{1}{2}x+2$, while the equation for Line 2 is $y=\nabla x-3$. What is the value of ∇ if the two lines are perpendicular?

44. The average yearly tuition to attend a private college increased at a relatively constant rate between 1980 and 2010. Use the graph shown to analyze this increase. All values are assumed to be rough estimates.

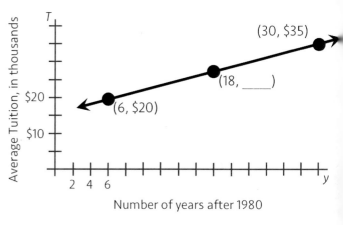

a. What was the average annual increase in the tuition between 1980 and 2010?

b. Fill in the blank shown in the graph and explain what this value means in the context of this scenario.

45. Refer to the graph on the previous scenario.

a. Write an equation that relates the average tuition T, measured in dollars, to the number of years, y, that have passed since 1980.

b. What was the average cost of yearly tuition in 1980?

c. Estimate the average cost of a private college tuition in 2015.

46. The table below represents a linear pattern. Identify the relationship between x and y.

x	0	1	2	3
y	-7	-2	3	8

47. ★Does the data in the table have a linear pattern? If it does, write an equation that shows how you can find a y-value if you have a given x-value.

x	-3	-1	2	6
y	39	33	24	12

Section 5
STANDARD FORM

When a linear equation is in Standard Form, it looks like Ax + By = C. To put this simply, the two variables are on the same side of the equation.

48. Consider the equation −6x + 5y = 30.

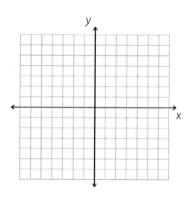

   a. If y is 0, what is the value of x?

   b. If x = 0, what is the value of y?

   c. Find another ordered pair that satisfies the equation.

   d. Graph the line formed by the equation −6x + 5y = 30.

49. Identify the x- and y- intercepts of the line formed by the equation 8x − 5y = 32.

50. Estimate the d- and g- intercepts of the line shown.

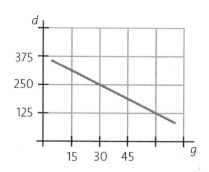

51. Consider the equation 3x − y = 6.

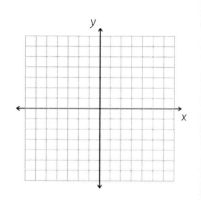

   a. Draw the graph for this equation by first locating the x- and y- intercepts.

   b. Is $(-2,-11.5)$ on the line?

52. When a linear function is written in the Standard Form, what is its typical structure?

53. What is the structure of a linear equation when it is in Slope-Intercept Form?

54. Write each equation in Standard Form. Clear the fractions to make A, B and C integers.

   a. $y = -2x + 7$

   b. $y = \frac{1}{4}x - 1$

   c. $x = -\frac{2}{5}y + \frac{7}{5}$

55. ★If $\frac{1}{3}x - \frac{1}{2}y = 7$, what is the value of $3y - 2x$?

56. Draw the 3 lines on the same graph. Plot points by using the strategy of plugging in 0 for one of the variables and solving for the other variable.

   a. $\frac{1}{12}x + \frac{1}{4}y = -\frac{1}{4}$

   b. $3.6x + 2.4y = 7.2$

   c. $-2x + 3y = 6$

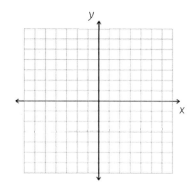

57. ★How can you prove that the triangle formed by the three lines in the previous scenario is a right triangle? It is not sufficient to say that it looks like a right triangle.

58. A rectangle has a length L and a width W.

   a. If the perimeter of the rectangle is 40 inches, write an equation that shows the relationship between L and W and the perimeter of the rectangle.

   b. If the perimeter of the rectangle is 40 inches, and the width is 4 inches less than twice the length, what are the dimensions of the rectangle?

59. In Finland, speeding tickets are calculated using an algorithm that matches the size of the fine with the driver's monthly income. The driver's monthly income is decreased by $235 and then the new total is divided by 60.

   a. Calculate the speeding ticket for someone who earns $10,000 per month.

   b. Write an equation that shows the relationship between the fine, F, and a driver's monthly income, i.

   ★c. Convert the equation to slope-intercept form, $F = mi + b$.

   ★d. What is the meaning of the i-intercept in the context of this scenario?

60. After earning $2,000 one summer, you decide to put your earnings into two accounts, one that will pay you 1% in interest for one year, and another that will pay you 4% in interest for one year. After one year, you earn $59 in interest. There are two equations that show relationships between the amounts of money invested, A and B, and the amount of interest earned that year. Determine these two equations and write them in Standard Form. Only write the equations.

61. Rewrite the following equation in Slope-Intercept Form.

$$y + 2 = -\frac{1}{3}(x + 6)$$

62. If a linear equation is in Standard Form, you can graph the line by setting up a T-chart and finding specific coordinates to plot. Describe two other methods by which you can graph a line when you start with an equation in Standard Form.

63. Identify the x- and y- intercepts of the line formed by the equation $-6x + 4y = -30$.

64. The line $3.6x + By = 24$ has a y-intercept at (0, 4.8). What is the value of B?

65. What is the x-intercept of the line described in the previous scenario?

Section 6
POINT-SLOPE FORM

66. Write the Point Slope Form for the equation of a line.

67. When a linear function is written in the Standard Form, what is its typical structure?

68. What is the structure of a linear equation when it is in Slope-Intercept Form?

69. If you forget the Point-Slope Form for a linear equation, what have you learned previously that you can use to derive the structure of this equation?

70. The equation $y+4=-\frac{5}{9}(x-27)$ forms a line containing the point (___, ___). The line's slope is ___.

71. The equation $y-19=-(x+30)$ forms a line that passes through the point (___, ___).

72. What is the slope of the line formed by the equation $y-\frac{2}{3}=-\left(x+\frac{1}{2}\right)$?

73. Given the following information, write the equation of the line in Point-Slope Form.

    a. The point $(5,2)$ is on the line and the slope of the line is $-\frac{2}{5}$.

    b. The point $(-1,-3)$ is on the line and the slope of the line is -1.

    c. The point $(0,-2)$ is on the line and the slope of the line is -2.

74. Rewrite each of the previous equations to convert them to Slope-Intercept Form.

75. Each of the equations below represents a line. The equations are written in such a way that they show one of the points on the line.

   a. The equation $y+8=\dfrac{1}{5}(x+10)$ passes through the point _____.

   b. The equation $y-20=-(x-4)$ passes through the point _____.

   c. The equation $y+200=-\dfrac{2}{7}(x-35)$ passes through the point _____.

76. Identify the slope of each line in the previous scenario.

77. Rewrite each of the previous 3 equations in Slope-Intercept Form.

78. Use the Point-Slope Form to write the equation of the line that contains the following points.

   a. $(1,-9)$ and $(4,0)$

   b. $(-2,3)$ and $(8,-5)$

79. Write an equation in Point-Slope Form that shows the relationship between M and t.

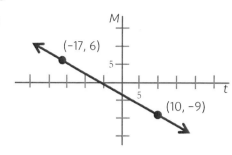

80. Draw the line for each equation shown below on the same graph.

   a. $y - 4 = -2(x + 2)$

   b. $y + 1 = \dfrac{3}{4}(x - 4)$

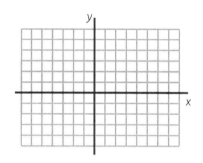

81. One of the three equations below does not belong with the other two. Which one?

   a. $y - 2 = -\dfrac{1}{2}(x - 10)$ b. $y - 5 = -\dfrac{1}{2}(x + 10)$ c. $y + 7 = -\dfrac{1}{2}(x - 14)$

82. Graph the previous three equations on the same Cartesian Plane. Label the axes as needed.

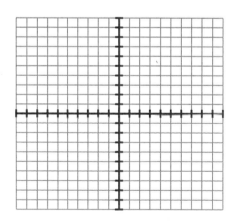

83. Write an equation for D in terms of t in Point-Slope Form.

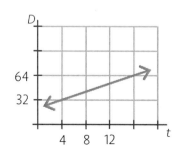

84. Rewrite the previous equation to convert it to Slope-Intercept Form.

85. The graph shows the change in the weight of a candle as it burns.

    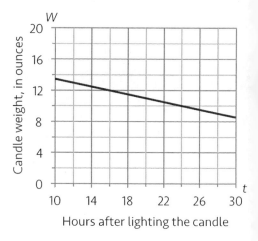

    a. Write an equation for W in terms of t in Point-Slope Form.

    b. Write an equation for W in terms of t in Slope-Intercept Form.

    c. What is the meaning of the W-intercept of the graph in the context of this scenario?

    d. What does the t-intercept mean in this scenario?

86. The cost of owning an inkjet printer can be hard to calculate. The price of the printer must be considered as well as the cost of the ink, which needs to be replaced when it runs out. An analysis of two printers is shown below.

    > A Canon Pixma printer costs $80. Based on the amount of pages that can be printed before the ink runs out, it costs 6 cents per page to own this printer.
    >
    > An HP Officejet printer costs $100, but its printing costs are only 2 cents per page.

    ★a. If you print an average of 80 pages per year, how many months will you need to own the HP printer before its overall costs are less than the overall cost of owning the Canon printer?

    b. How many pages would you need to print before the overall cost of owning the HP printer is less than the Canon printer?

87. The graph displays how the boiling point of water changes as the elevation changes.

a. If you are heating water at sea level (an elevation of 0 feet), what temperature does the water need to reach before it will start boiling?

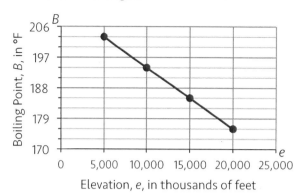

★b. By how many degrees does the boiling point of water decrease when your elevation increases by 1000 feet?

c. Write an equation for the line shown in the graph. Use the variables B and e, where B is the boiling point of water at an elevation of e feet. Write your equation in Point-Slope Form.

88. You have now learned how to write linear equations in 3 different forms, but it is easy to mix these up when you try to remember them. Write the three equation forms below.

a. Slope-Intercept Form
b. Standard Form
c. Point-Slope Form

89. Graph the line without changing the equation.

$$y+3=\frac{2}{3}(x+6)$$

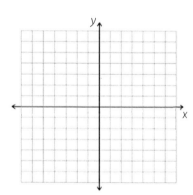

90. A printing machine is set up to print 1000 posters. It takes 8 minutes to print 300 posters. How much longer will it take for the printer to finish the entire job if it continues printing at the same rate?

Section 7
AN INTRODUCTION TO TREND LINES

HOMEWORK & EXTRA PRACTICE SCENARIOS

91. Lego sets come in many different sizes. Some sets contain less than 100 Lego pieces, while larger sets can contain more than 1,000 pieces. The graph below shows the prices for various Lego sets, as observed at a local toy store.

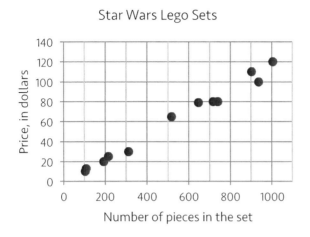

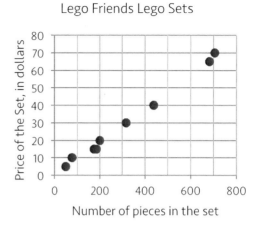

a. Which variety of Lego sets has a higher price per piece, Star Wars or Lego Friends?

b. Draw a trend line through the points in each data set above and identify the equation of your trend line.

c. How does your work in part b. help you answer the question in part a.?

92. ★A pedometer is a tool that counts how many steps you take. It uses this number to guess how many miles you have traveled. The table below shows data from Kabir's pedometer as he checks it throughout the day.

a. If Kabir walked 6 miles, how many steps did he take, according to the pedometer?

b. Estimate the equation of the trend line that passes through the data points.

93. ★Kabir's stride length is the distance he travels when he takes 1 step. In the previous scenario, how long is Kabir's stride length, according to the pedometer? Write the length in feet. (1 mile = 5,280 ft)

94. The bar graph displays a small data set.

    a. What scenario does this data describe?

    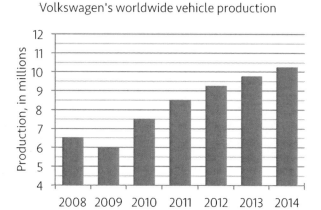

    b. Draw an approximate trend line through the bar graph shown.

    c. Find the equation of your trend line, in Point-Slope Form. Use P for the total vehicle production, and y for the year.

95. In the previous scenario, what was the average increase in the number of vehicles produced each year over the time period shown?

96. Eleven kids walk into a frozen yogurt store. At this store, they get a bowl and they can fill it with as much frozen yogurt and toppings as they would like. The price is calculated by weighing the entire mixture. Estimate the cost of the yogurt, in dollars per ounce.

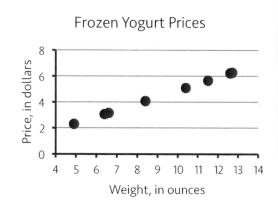

97. The table shows the number of Facebook users worldwide from 2009 to 2014.

Year, y	Users, U, in millions
2009	360
2010	608
2011	845
2012	1,056
2013	1,229
2014	1,393

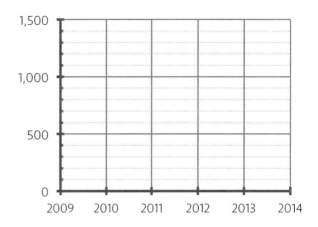

a. Create a scatter plot for the data.

b. Draw a trend line through the data and find its equation to show the relationship between U and y.

98. Use your work in the previous scenario to answer the following questions

a. What was the average increase in users per year?

b. Estimate the number of users in 2015.

c. Can you rely on your equation to predict the number of worldwide users in 2050?

99. The data in the graph shown displays how the weight of a car affects its gas mileage. Draw a trend line and find the equation of your line to approximate the relationship between a car's gas mileage, M, and its weight, w.

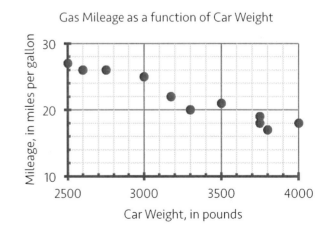

Gas Mileage as a function of Car Weight

HOMEWORK & EXTRA PRACTICE SCENARIOS

100. ★Use your work in the previous scenario to answer the following questions.

   a. Estimate the gas mileage for a car that weighs 2000 pounds.

   b. According to your trend line, how does a 500 lb. weight increase affect the gas mileage?

101. ★Your city participates in a recycling program that allows you to accumulate points based on the number of pounds of recycling that you set aside each week. The table below shows the number of points you have earned based on the number of weeks you have been participating in the program.

Weeks in the Program	6	12	20	24	34
Points Earned	35,000	80,000	110,000	150,000	200,000

   a. If you can trade in your points for prizes, how many weeks will you need to participate in the program in order to earn a prize worth 325,000 points?

   b. Estimate the number of points you earn per pound if you have recycled a total of 750 pounds after 30 weeks.

102. Does the data in each graph shown an upward trend or a downward trend?

a. 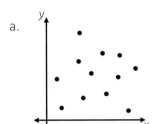 b. 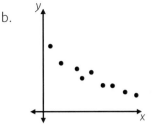 c.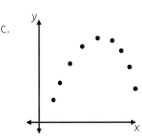

103. Graph two lines, Line 1 and Line 2, using the restrictions below.

   Line 1 contains the point (−3, 5).

   The lines intersect at (6, 2)

   The lines are perpendicular.

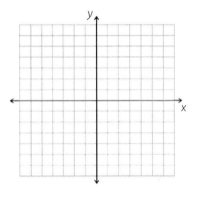

Section 8
VERTICAL AND HORIZONTAL LINES

104. Select two ordered pairs from the solid line shown and find its slope.

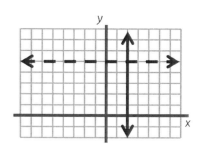

a. What do you notice?

b. Now select two ordered pairs from the dashed line and find the slope of this line. What do you notice?

105. What is the slope of a horizontal line? Explain why a horizontal line has this particular slope?

106. What is the slope of a vertical line? Explain why a vertical line has this particular slope?

107. Two lines are shown on the Cartesian Plane to the right.

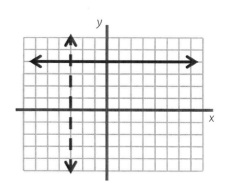

a. Identify the equation of the dashed line.

b. Identify the equation of the solid line.

108. Graph the lines formed by the following equations.

a. $x = -6$

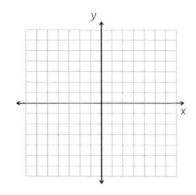

b. $y = 7$

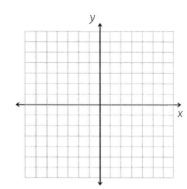

109. Graph the line formed by the equation below.

$$2x - 3y = -3(x + y)$$

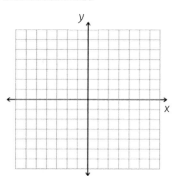

110. Graph the lines shown below on the same Cartesian Plane.

   a. $y = -\dfrac{1}{2}x + 2.5$

   b. $x = 5$

   c. $y = 4$

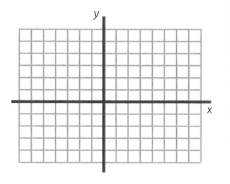

111. Calculate the area of the region bordered by the three lines in the previous scenario.

112. Graph the lines shown below on the same Cartesian Plane.

   a. $y - 3 = -2(x + 2)$

   b. $x = 2$

   c. $y = \dfrac{3}{4}x + 4.5$

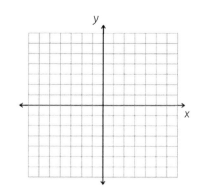

113. Calculate the area of the region bordered by the three lines in the previous scenario.

Section 9
LINEAR INEQUALITIES

HOMEWORK & EXTRA PRACTICE SCENARIOS

When you graph an inequality, there are two steps involved. First, you draw a boundary line. Then, you shade one side of the line to show the solution region for the inequality.

114. Part of an inequality is shown below. The boundary line for the inequality is also shown. State which side of the line you shade to finish the graph of the inequality.

    a. $y \leq$ _____   b. $y >$ _____   c. $x \geq$ _____

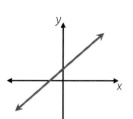
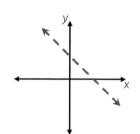
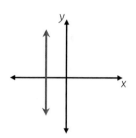

115. Use the word <u>positive</u> or <u>negative</u> to describe the slope of each of the lines shown in the previous scenario.

116. Once again, part of an inequality is shown below. The boundary line for the inequality is also shown. State which side of the line you shade to finish the graph of the inequality.

    a. $y \geq$ _____   b. $x <$ _____   c. $y \leq$ _____

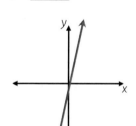
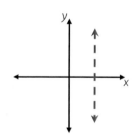
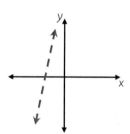

117. Use the word positive or negative to describe the slope of each of the lines in the previous scenario.

118. Plot all of the points that form the solution to the inequality $y \geq -4$.

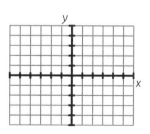

119. Plot all of the points that form the solution to the inequality $x \leq 2$.

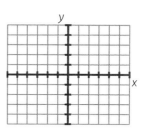

120. Graph the given inequality.

a. $y < 0$
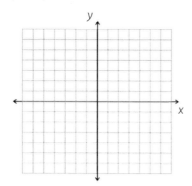

b. $x > 0$
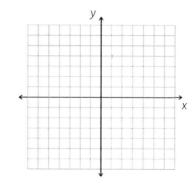

121. Write the inequality that has the solution set shown in each graph below.

a.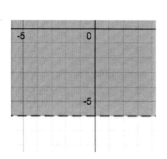

b.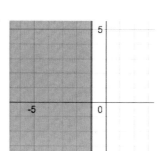

c.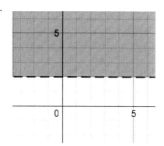

122. Graph the solution region for each inequality shown.

a. $y \leq -\dfrac{1}{4}x + 2$
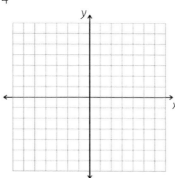

b. $y > -3x - 1$
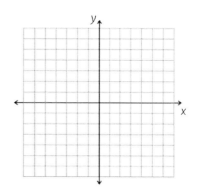

123. Write the inequality that has the solution set shown in each graph below.

a.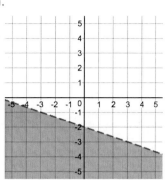

b.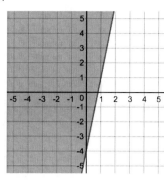

c.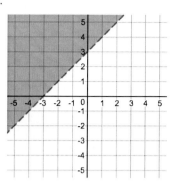

124. Is the ordered pair (0,0) located in the solution region for each of the inequalities shown?

   a. $y > -2x + 7$
   b. $y \leq -x$
   c. $-3x + 4y < 12$
   d. $-3x + \frac{2}{7}y > 4$

125. Is the ordered pair (6, −15) located in the solution region for the inequality shown?

$$\frac{1}{2}x - \frac{3}{5}y > 12$$

126. Without graphing, is the ordered pair (1, −4) located in the solution region for either of the inequalities shown in the next scenario?

127. In each of the graphs below, mark the solution region for the inequality shown.

a. $x - y \leq 5$
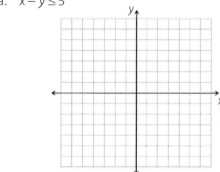

b. $y < -4x$
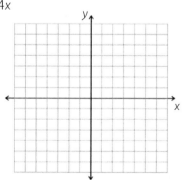

128. Without graphing, is the ordered pair (−4,0) located in the solution region for either of the inequalities shown in the next scenario?

129. Graph the inequality shown.

$-2x - 4y \geq 8$

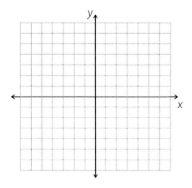

130. Graph the inequality shown.

$2y + x > -2(2 - y)$

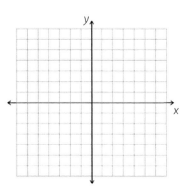

131. Christopher Mele wrote an article about waiting in line at the supermarket. In this article, he quotes Dan Meyer, "Every person requires a fixed amount of time to say hello, pay, say goodbye and clear out of the lane." In his research, Dan Meyer found that the average person takes about 41 seconds plus an additional 3 seconds per item to get through the lane when they are trying to pay for all of their items. (https://www.nytimes.com/2016/09/08/business/how-to-pick-the-fastest-line-at-the-supermarket.html)

   a. Given this average, how long does it take for someone to wait in line if they are standing behind someone who has 40 items in their cart?

   b. Lane 1 has 4 people in it who each have 5 items in their cart. Lane 2 has 1 person in it with 20 items in their cart. Which lane would you choose if you want to get through quickly?

Section 10
CUMULATIVE REVIEW

132. One line is shown in the graph. Draw a second line that runs perpendicular to the line shown and passes through the point (−2, 6).

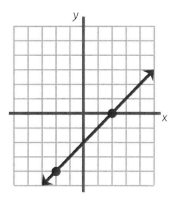

   a. Write the equation of the second line in Point-Slope Form.

   b. Write both equations in Slope-Intercept Form.

133. Write an equation of a line that is parallel to the graph of $-4x+2y=6$ and has the same y-intercept as the graph of $2y+3x=-6$. Graph all 3 of the lines to confirm your accuracy.

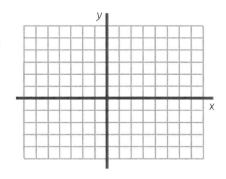

134. In the graph to the right, imagine that you can lift the line off of the page and move it around. If you slide the line down 3 units, where will the line cross the y-axis after you have moved it?

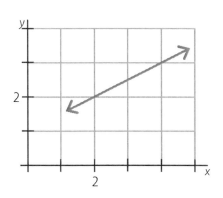

135. If $3^2 + 3^2 + 3^2 = 3^x$, what is the value of X?

136. In previous lessons, you learned that $\sqrt{A^2}$ can be simplified as A, if $A \geq 0$. Is it also true that the expression $\sqrt{A^2 + B^2}$ has the same value as $A+B$? In order to help you determine if this is true, evaluate $\sqrt{A^2 + B^2}$ using $A = 8$ and $B = 6$.

137. Without using a ruler, draw a triangle with side lengths 5cm, 5cm, and 8cm. Use the line segment shown below as a guide to help you, but focus more on the general shape of this triangle rather than trying to draw your line segments with the exact measurements.

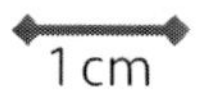

1 cm

138. ★Calculate the area of the triangle in the previous scenario.

Section 11
ANSWER KEY

1.	a. $x = 12$ b. $x = 19.5$ c. $x = 27$
2.	a. $x = 12$ b. $x = 12$ c. $x = 12$
3.	a. multiply by 3 b. multiply by 8 c. multiply by 20
4.	a. $x - 15 = 13$ b. $5x - 14 = 20$ c. $6x - 24 = 15x + 30$
5.	a. $y = \dfrac{2}{3}x + 2$ b. $y = -\dfrac{3}{2}x + 3$
6.	$y = -\dfrac{1}{3}x - 1$
7.	a. $(-7,5)$ b. $(3,4)$ c. $(-6,-3)$ d. $(6,0)$ e. $(0,0)$ f. $(0,-4)$ g. $(8,-5)$
8.	Point #2 (the point with an x-value closer to 0 is closer to the y-axis)
9.	Each point is equidistant from $(0, 0)$. All 3 points are exactly 5 units away from $(0, 0)$. You can confirm this using the Pythagorean Theorem $\to a^2 + b^2 = c^2$.
10.	a. $400,000 b. $175,000
11.	a. December b. Feb., Oct., Nov.
12.	a. Oct. & Nov. b. Jun. & Jul. and Jul. & Aug.
13.	a. positive b. negative c. neither (its slope is "0")
14.	a. $\dfrac{2}{3}$ b. -2
15.	a. Pearl b. Pearl took the longest amount of time to travel the distance c. 0.08 meters per sec. (12 m in 150 sec.)
16.	a. they earn the same amount b. $12/hr
17.	$\dfrac{y_2 - y_1}{x_2 - x_1}$ or $\dfrac{y_1 - y_2}{x_1 - x_2}$
18.	a. slope $= \dfrac{24 - 4}{6 - (-10)} = \dfrac{20}{16} = \dfrac{5}{4}$
19.	a. slope $= \dfrac{3 - (-12)}{-10 - 5} = \dfrac{15}{-15} = -1$ b. slope $= \dfrac{8 - (-3)}{101 - 101} = \dfrac{11}{0} =$ undefined
20.	a. $-\dfrac{4}{3}$ b. -1
21.	$K = -2$
22.	$2y = 5x + 10 \to y = \dfrac{5}{2}x + 5 \to$ slope is $\dfrac{5}{2}$
23.	$-10y = -3x + 40 \to y = \dfrac{3}{10}x - 4 \to$ slope is $\dfrac{3}{10}$
24.	$y = mx + b$
25.	$y = \dfrac{1}{3}x - 2$
26.	a. Yes b. No
27.	If the equation $y = \dfrac{4}{5}x - 1$ is true when $x = -15$ and $y = -13$, then the point satisfies the equation.
28.	$D = -12t + 720$
29.	Rewrite equation: $9x + 9y = 45 \to y = -x + 5$
30.	a & b. [graph] c. The lines are perpendicular because their slopes are opposite reciprocals.
31.	$(0, 25) \to y = 7x + b \to 11 = 7(-2) + b \to b = 25$
32.	$(0, -17)$ $y = \dfrac{5}{6}x + b \to -7 = \dfrac{5}{6}(12) + b \to b = -17$
33.	solid: $(0, 3)$ dashed: $(0, -6)$
34.	solid: $y = \dfrac{1}{3}x + 3$ dashed: $y = x - 6$

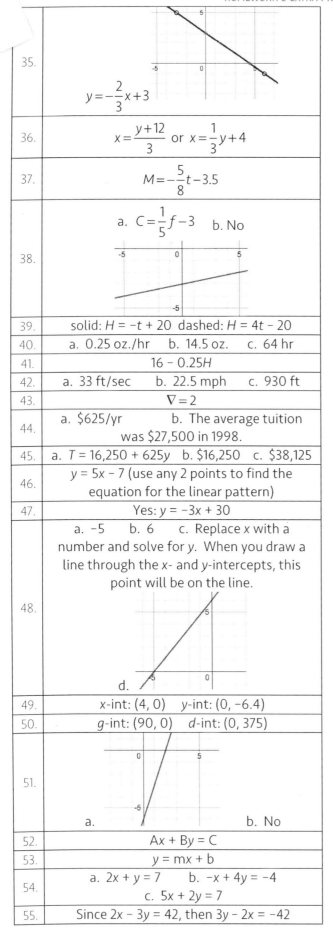

	c. $y = -\frac{2}{7}x - 190$
78.	a. $y+9=3(x-1)$ or $y=3(x-4)$ b. $y-3=-\frac{4}{5}(x+2)$ or $y+5=-\frac{4}{5}(x-8)$
79.	$M-6=-\frac{5}{9}(t+17)$ or $M+9=-\frac{5}{9}(t-10)$
80.	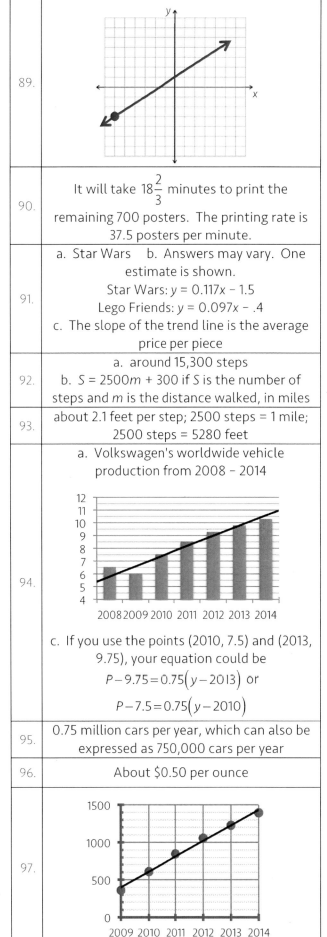
81.	$y-2=-\frac{1}{2}(x-10)$
82.	
83.	$D-32=\frac{8}{3}(t-4)$ or $D-64=\frac{8}{3}(t-16)$
84.	$y=\frac{8}{3}x+\frac{64}{3}$
85.	a. $W-12=-\frac{1}{4}(t-16)$ b. $W=-\frac{1}{4}t+16$ c. The weight of the candle when it starts burning d. The time it takes for the candle to burn down completely
86.	a. 75 months b. more than 500 pages $100+0.02p<80+0.06p \rightarrow p>500$
87.	a. 212°F b. 1.8° (it decreases 9° for every 5000 ft increase in elevation) c. Many options: $B-203=-\frac{9}{5,000}(x-5,000)$, $B-194=-0.0018(x-10,000)$, etc.
88.	a. $y=mx+b$ b. $Ax+By=C$ c. $y-y_1=m(x-x_1)$
89.	
90.	It will take $18\frac{2}{3}$ minutes to print the remaining 700 posters. The printing rate is 37.5 posters per minute.
91.	a. Star Wars b. Answers may vary. One estimate is shown. Star Wars: $y = 0.117x - 1.5$ Lego Friends: $y = 0.097x - .4$ c. The slope of the trend line is the average price per piece
92.	a. around 15,300 steps b. $S = 2500m + 300$ if S is the number of steps and m is the distance walked, in miles
93.	about 2.1 feet per step; 2500 steps = 1 mile; 2500 steps = 5280 feet
94.	a. Volkswagen's worldwide vehicle production from 2008 – 2014 c. If you use the points (2010, 7.5) and (2013, 9.75), your equation could be $P-9.75=0.75(y-2013)$ or $P-7.5=0.75(y-2010)$
95.	0.75 million cars per year, which can also be expressed as 750,000 cars per year
96.	About $0.50 per ounce
97.	

	b. If you use the points (2010, 608) and (2013, 1229), your equation could be $U - 1229 = 207(y - 2013)$	110.	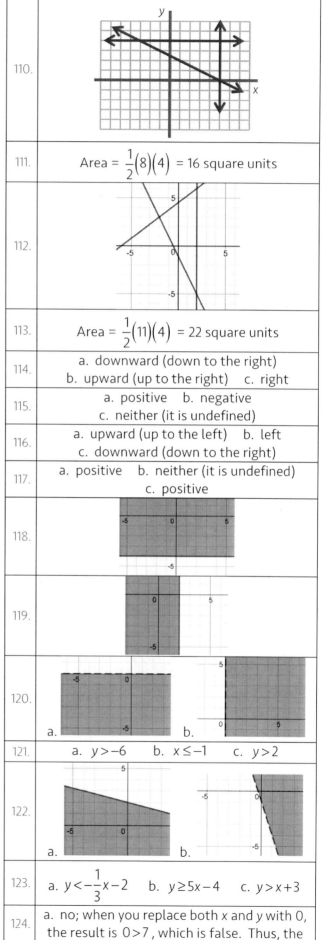
98.	a. 207 million users per year b. 1.643 billion users c. only if the current trend continues in a linear pattern		
99.	a. If you use the points (2750, 26) and (3750, 18), your equation could be $M - 26 = -0.008(w - 2750)$	111.	Area $= \frac{1}{2}(8)(4)$ = 16 square units
		112.	
100.	a. 32 miles per gallon (mpg) b. gas mileage would decrease by 4 mpg	113.	Area $= \frac{1}{2}(11)(4)$ = 22 square units
101.	possible trend line: $y = 5893x - 362$ a. ≈55 weeks b. ≈240 points per pound	114.	a. downward (down to the right) b. upward (up to the right) c. right
102.	a. no trend b. downward c. no trend	115.	a. positive b. negative c. neither (it is undefined)
103.		116.	a. upward (up to the left) b. left c. downward (down to the right)
		117.	a. positive b. neither (it is undefined) c. positive
		118.	
104.	a. the slope is undefined b. the slope is 0	119.	
105.	A horizontal line has a slope of 0, because it does not "rise." A fraction of $\frac{0}{\text{nonzero}}$ has a value of 0.	120.	a. b.
106.	A vertical line has an undefined slope, because it does not "run." A fraction of $\frac{\text{nonzero}}{0}$ is undefined.	121.	a. $y > -6$ b. $x \leq -1$ c. $y > 2$
107.	a. $x = -3$ b. $y = 4$	122.	a. b.
108.	a. b.	123.	a. $y < -\frac{1}{3}x - 2$ b. $y \geq 5x - 4$ c. $y > x + 3$
109.	Rewrite the equation as $x = 0$. Graph a vertical line that traces the y-axis	124.	a. no; when you replace both x and y with 0, the result is $0 > 7$, which is false. Thus, the

125.	point (0,0) is not in the solution region of the inequality. b. yes; $0 \leq 0$ is true c. yes, $0 < 12$ is true d. no, $0 > 4$ is false no, $12 > 12$ is false $\frac{1}{2}(6) - \frac{3}{5}(-15) > 12 \rightarrow 3 + 9 > 12$
126.	a. yes, $5 \leq 5$ is true b. no, $-4 < -4$ is false
127.	a. (graph) b. (graph)
128.	a. yes, $8 \geq 8$ is true b. no, $-4 > -4$ is false
129.	$-4y \geq 2x + 8 \rightarrow y \leq -\frac{1}{2}x - 2$ (graph)
130.	$2y + x > -4 + 2y \rightarrow x > -4$ (graph)

131.	a. $41 + 3(40) \rightarrow 161$ seconds $\rightarrow$ 2 min, 41 sec. b. Lane 2 is 123 sec. faster (almost 2 min) Lane 1: 224 seconds $41 + 3(5) + 41 + 3(5) + 41 + 3(5) + 41 + 3(5)$ Lane 2: 101 seconds $\rightarrow 41 + 3(20)$
132.	a. $y - 6 = -(x + 2)$ b. $y = -x + 4$ and $y = x - 2$
133.	$y = 2x - 3$
134.	$(0, -2)$
135.	$x = 3$
136.	No.
137.	(triangle figure)
138.	The height is 3 cm (use the Pythagorean Theorem), which makes the area 12 cm^2.

Made in United States
North Haven, CT
18 March 2023